STUDENT OF LIFE

Why Becoming Engaged in Life, Art, and Philosophy Can Lead to a Happier Existence

Brannon W. McConkey

abbott press®
A DIVISION OF WRITER'S DIGEST

Abbott Press books may be ordered through booksellers or by contacting:

Abbott Press
1663 Liberty Drive
Bloomington, IN 47403
www.abbottpress.com
Phone: 1-866-697-5310

Because of the dynamic nature of the Internet, any web addresses or links contained in this book may have changed since publication and may no longer be valid. The views expressed in this work are solely those of the author and do not necessarily reflect the views of the publisher, and the publisher hereby disclaims any responsibility for them.

Cover photographs by Brannon W. McConkey

Contact the author at Blues_is_forever@hotmail.com

ISBN: 978-1-4582-1427-0 (sc)
ISBN: 978-1-4582-1428-7 (e)

Library of Congress Control Number: 2014902740

Printed in the United States of America.

Abbott Press rev. date: 02/14/2014

CONTENTS

PREFACE

I sat and watched inquisitively as the smoke from my cigarette floated languidly into the crisp night sky. This tobacco smoke, as if possessing its own capacity for philosophical understanding, climbed peacefully, slowly twisting and turning, as if with prehensile-like arms toward its desired destination. It was where it needed to be and was going where it needed to go. It was quiet. The stillness was a bit stifling. There was no confusion or bumbling or faltering. There was no mystification. There was only quiet certainty.

Now, this was obviously my personification of an insensate thing. I was projecting my own incertitude, confusion, and frustration onto the world around me. This smoke really has it together. Why can't I achieve the same decided comfort? How evidently easy it is simply to be at peace. This smoke is on to something.

I momentarily missed the interesting fact that my ascription of peace, harmony, understanding, and happiness to this sage-like smoke was ultimately the byproduct of burning a cancer stick. Moments of clarity are often enmeshed in the farcical and ironic. Lucidity and understanding are sometimes entrenched in absurd tapestries of ideas and events. Such is life.

Life can also be simple, even if it isn't often simply understood. A quotidian philosophy can be easily developed by almost anyone. Indeed, most of our heavy intellectual and emotional lifting is done in the most profoundly banal circumstances. (I say, with slight humor, consider the toilet).

Many authors might wax eloquently about the rising smoke from their expensive Cuban cigar, as they write from some luxurious, privileged enclave – perhaps a majestic beach or canyon, or some similar envy-provoking holdout. Not this author. Let me paint you a picture: I sit under an oppressively dim, Orwellian-invoking street lamp hovering menacingly above, which was strategically placed in my back yard. My wife and I rent from a retired electrical lineman – a person with a dangerous vocation. He would repair obstructed or destructed electrical lines caused by a storm or adventurous (and concomitantly dead) animal. This burly and simplistically wise old retiree installed this lamp to illuminate the shadowy back yard. (The streetlamps in front of the house were not quite sufficient in their illumination.) I occupy a weather-ridden, slightly rusty, black metal chair. This sits on an aged concrete patio that is surrounded by an unkempt "garden" area (which, I admit, is from my lack of attending to it). All of this in a ridiculously pedestrian, tightly organized neighborhood, built in the 60's (picture the one-story, monochromatic scene), dwelling in unabashed, suburban mediocrity. I live, smoke, and write this from an avowedly uninspired enclave of my own (comparatively speaking, here).

I sit and light up this smoke, watching its contents unfold, just so I can enjoy letting my mind freely wander. It took me a while to decide whether or not that was sad, if not somewhat ridiculous. I don't even "smoke." But, at that time – the time I also decided that writing a book might not be such a bad idea – watching this smoke, like an inspired whirling dervish dancing toward the sky, produced as serene and lucid a moment that I reasonably could have hoped for. In this case, or at any rate, I couldn't admonish myself too much for personifying smoke or burning a cancer stick.

That is as modest as it can be. True moments of clarity can come in the light of – or in spite of – simplicity. I did not need to paint a resplendent picture of untouchable beauty or rarity – like our envied, hypothetical, cigar-smoking author (it would have been untrue at any rate). I sat poor, probably unshaven, and watched as my humdrum cancer stick burned intently in the opaque night. Can you imagine a more uninspiring event? The point on which to take note is my full *immersion* or *engagement* in my activity - not the *smoking*, but what it produced. This is what truly matters in living a happy, sustainable life; or, at least a life that attempts to maximize happiness. And why wouldn't that be an important goal?

My opening offers a good anecdote to display my point about this book, but it certainly isn't the only moment. Understanding our lives – and what we can do to maximize happiness and understanding – can occur in unsuspecting moments at any given time. We should not, however, be passive bystanders. Fully engaging ourselves with and in these experiences can give us an unwavering confidence – whether we be poor or rich, unshaven or debonair, provincial or cosmopolitan, or busy or free – to grab our lives by the tail, smile at them (pardon a trite cliché), and change what we want to change. To know when and how to study each moment, actively engaged, is the picture I intend to paint for you with this book. There are many ways to do this, many avenues to discover, and I spend the rest of the book laying this out and driving this home. It really matters.

The take home message, then, is that if you don't yet smoke you should probably go ahead and start (relax, Dr. Phil, I'm kidding). Prolific writer and contrarian, Christopher Hitchens, once wryly quipped: "I think everyone has a book in them. And in most people that is where it should stay." I hope the need for writing this book will be self-evident in the pages to come. (And, if any of this is confusing, I suggest you quickly purchase the book and read on for further elucidation.) It was coming out of me anyway, even if it should have stayed there. At any rate I thank you, Dear Reader, for taking the time even thus far to read these words, and I sincerely hope you and your life are the better for it.

(If not, you should probably at least forget about that whole smoking bit.)

Brannon McConkey
Shelbyville, TN
07/6/13

INTRODUCTION

> We shall not cease from exploration
> And the end of all our exploring
> Will be to arrive where we started
> And know the place for the first time
> T.S. Elliot from *Little Gidding*

I can't promise during the course of this book that I will not blithely toss out ambiguous clichés. But I will give it the old college try. You know the (Dickensian) type. I won't tell you it was the best of times or the worst of times (or more presumptuous yet, the best *and* worst of times – a brazen claim, to be sure). I will not produce gross generalizations and platitudes: life is beautiful/life stinks. Although this book has a certain vagueness and incertitude – and rather is open and subject to those types of cheap eye-grabbers – the content in these pages is not meant to be a panacea or fix-all.

This is decidedly not a "self-help" or "self-improvement" book. Many of those books are dime store knock-offs, peddling cheap truisms and platitudes, and feed directly into your already richly prepared, gullible mentality. And the term "life coach" is laughable – as if we develop some set of whiteboard plays for our "team" to employ. They tell you exactly what you want to hear (or think you need to hear). You invariably hear things like this: "With determination and will, you can succeed!" or "Follow your heart/gut hunch!" How evidently emphatic they are about their advice! It fits right on the poster! Who wouldn't be excited?

But what do those phrases really mean? Has anyone reading this *not* succeeded with an ostensibly copious amount of determination and will? Everyone should be nodding their heads. It matters not how iron the will or unflinching the determination – sometimes things just don't "work out." It is obvious upon hearing it, yet people sort of glaze over and lose their discriminating abilities as soon as they run into such vapid pep-talkery. The heart? The heart is a pump circulating blood through the body. My "gut" is where my breakfast burrito goes. My gut is now apparently also "hunching?"

Now, you may laugh (if you didn't, you aren't reading it correctly) and say, "Well…true. But you know what they mean." I do know what they are trying to say. But I do not see it as a harmless dumbing down of general information. First off, it *is* generally known – and *easily* understood – information. This is why people move *en masse* to purchase a book telling them as much (so little is the work required to make us feel good about "doing something.") But the information isn't true. It is a string of fatuous truisms, tautologies, and non-sequiturs. The information tells everyone what they would like to hear. The authors are effectual "yes men". Much like the interaction with a "conveyor of spirits," though, people can and are emotionally hurt when the desired or expected outcome is not there (or, in the case of the pernicious "spirit medium," *is* there). In other words, we want to hear what we want to hear and are selective about doing so. Even when we feel the inevitable pangs of defeat, we head right back to the source of the trouble like unchanging and abject slaves, prostrating to a master. This master, though, has only the power you ascribe to him.

So, my book, then, is simultaneously both the antithesis of, and similar to, the aforementioned quackery and hucksterism.

This, in some sense, is the *sine qua non* of the book – and life. Philosophical contradictions make things both more difficult and more beautiful. Life *can* be beautiful, and life *can* stink. It can be both the *best* and *worst* of times. And sometimes this fact simply cannot be avoided.

If, at this point, you wish to put down the book because the answers you were after are not black and white or Manichean in nature, I will understand. Truly understanding and appreciating life requires this admission - the admission of possible uncertainty, confusion, ignorance, fear and change. This is the incontrovertible truth about life. There is no quick fix, single pill, six-minute abs version of the few decades we have on the planet. Living happily requires nuance, subtlety, and persistent questioning. A comfortable life requires paying close attention to language and reactions. What are we *really* saying, and why are we reacting the way we do? Why do we feel this way? Do we even know? Why do we *feel* at all?

If the title and subtitle grabbed you then you probably formulated a question from them. How can I become more engaged in life and why does it matter? Add to that the somewhat confusing, slightly annoying array of questions and points raised in this introduction. If you care about this sort of thing – and have read this far – you are in luck because I will answer these questions, address these points, and hopefully proceed to help you live a happier, more thorough existence. Just keep in mind this won't come by way of facile aphorism or pithy formulations. We have to put in some philosophical grunt work.

Ok, on with it then. The book is laid out as follows. There are three main parts of this book, and also an additional section addressing possible criticisms of or concerns about my arguments. The first section is the Philosophy part. It is the longest and most meaty section. This consists of several (at least partially integrated) arguments, observations, and ideas about what to expect – or what one *should* expect – from life. Some of the points, observations and ideas (which are broken into "chapters" within the section) also paint vivid imagery of what *not* do or expect or deduce from life. It forces some of the big questions. Some of the themes include: being in control, the critical importance of paying attention to our language, thinking about time, our quest for immortality, reflecting upon nature and simplicity, and understanding history and our interconnected past. This section (if I may) is the mind-altering, game-changing one; the one that helps you get your mind and life on steady, peaceful pavement. You are henceforward equipped with proper working machinery and new wheels.

Once the backbone is laid out, section two gives examples of art or artistic endeavors to pursue. I could have stopped after explaining and arguing the large philosophical points (well… had I done that I technically would not have had book-length information to provide. Then you would be reading a life-altering pamphlet). I want to offer you individual examples of things in which to become engaged and immersed. The list I give – which includes lifelong and diverse hobbies such as photography, cooking, and Brazilian jiu-jitsu – is meant to provide a jumping off point. You, then, Dear Reader, will have a veritable buffet of life-changing options. The arts or artistic pursuits I have included are not new, but the way I dissect and let you peer into and scrutinize them allow for an engagement that can be life-altering. Along with new wheels you will henceforward have an open road and an itinerary of your choosing. If I may indulge a bit, your life can now "get back on track." (I can't let the dime store hacks and charlatans have *all* the fun.)

The last section I use to explain one last general idea. It is about bridging the gap between art (and philosophy, and other artsy stuff) and science. I write about how there is a false dichotomy proposed over science and art. The seemingly ineradicable wedge between art and science is, as I argue, a non-issue. I also take the time in this section to address the importance of science in our lives, and how everyone can both think "realistically" and live in the "real word" while still finding time to become engaged in philosophical and artistic pursuits. In many ways this is the most important section because of its recourse to most people's practical sensibilities. Don't fear, Dear Reader, as I spend time with these concerns as well. Your new car is on the road, your map is of your choosing, and analogously, you have money in your pocket and a spare tire (practical sensibilities, folks).

The last main section leads into a subsequent section addressing potential legitimate criticisms and concerns about my content. This is an important section for anyone arguing, well, anything. (Perhaps we should pass this news on to politicians?)

And then, lastly, I deliver my dénouement – my signature *coup de maître*. Put more simply, the conclusion. This is obviously the section preceding your ardent recommendation of my book to friends and family. If, for some inconceivable reason, you do not like the book you may give it to a friend. (By the way, I will need to see a receipt of purchase.)

With jest aside, I do sincerely thank you, my Dear Reader (as I will lovingly and repeatedly refer to you all throughout these pages), not just for reading my book and considering its content, but for merely existing. That is all it takes to start living life engaged in the beauty and splendor around us. We just need to be ever vigilant. Ok, then. That's it. Off you go.

Only that day dawns to which we are awake
- Henry David Thoreau *Walden*

PART 1

THE PHILOSOPHY

CH. 1 CURLED LIP SYNDROME

Philosophy can sound a little scary to those who are not settled with the term. Isn't that just the class those uppity college kids take at university? The class they learn about a lot of useless abstract thinking? Don't sell any philosophy at my doorstep. No soliciting – I'm all set, thanks. I can see your face now. It's a bit curled, and your brow is furrowed. Socrates, right? That philosophy? Got something to do with Ancient Greece? What the hell has that got to do with me? Make it quick, because American Idol is about to return...

That image – the image of some old people and old ideas steeped in old ass antiquity – is not *wrong*, but there is so much more to it. A history of philosophy would of course include Socrates (a class without Socrates would certainly be a shitty one). After all, he was the one who turned our philosophical gaze on *ourselves*. Previously, philosophy had been concerned over the nature of the cosmos (a fine pursuit itself). But what does philosophy have to do with you right now?

When I was in high school in rural Bell Buckle, Tennessee back in the first couple of years of the 21st century, I took a philosophy class that awoke me from a cognitive slumber. I entered back into that slumber in my college days, but the spark was lit and my interest in life and thought was simply lying dormant. I admit that I had an initial interest in what the class may offer. I had to take another elective anyway. It was either that or underwater basket weaving – a crossroads decision that I may yet still come to regret. ("You'll rue the day!" intoned the basket-weaving professor.) You imagine that a class like this unfolds as follows: an unwavering British professor walks in with bow tie, ruler in hand, and curled upper lip. The students, slightly cowered, sit in silent, stolid reticence. Professor curled lip then proceeds to bore all students into oblivion.

My class, however, was an amazingly open forum for discussing all of the wildest ideas we could imagine: can we *really* know a thing-in-itself, or can we only know our perceptions of it? What is the mind's role in assessing our actions? Are our minds and brains the *same thing*? What is the role of religion in society? What is the role of politics in society? Is the world completely *material* or is there something of the *numinous* "there" somewhere? Philosophy isn't just an exercise in the abstract. There are more basic questions to cover as well. How do we live in a functioning society together? Can we be good to each other on a permanent basis, and if so how would we do that? Aren't we all really the same in some important sense? And more rudimentary still: should we bother considering philosophy in the midst of a "normal life?"

The last question is one I attempt to answer. It is the most salient and pertinent question for us. It is the first question we should (and typically do) ask. The answer is *yes*. Very rarely do we *truly* answer big questions in philosophy; we only increase the amount of questions (which means we are doing it right). In this case, though, there is an answer to the question, and it is an emphatic *yes*.

It isn't that we are *doing* philosophy or even studying it, but that we are just living life philosophically. What do I mean by that? Most people do *some* of this without realizing it. We are living life *engaged* in our surroundings, in other people, and in our thoughts and activities (and the thoughts and activities of others). Imagine simply being a bystander to life. This is what many people assuredly do. They do not realize, but they have been sucked into the black hole of complacency and stasis. The implications of this are important, so we should take a moment to think about this. Considering the implications of *anything* is a promising first step on the road out of the morass of humdrum living. I picture a sort of zombie here, so I use the term "living" with slight wryness.

My college days were not, I would posit, an altogether exemplary model for zombie living (I did ok for myself) – but they were not too far off. Perhaps I am being too critical of myself. I did well in school. I worked a little bit (the obligatory retail position). I had a few hobbies, had several friends, and frequently romanticized and charmed (gentlemanly, no?). Only later, upon engaged reflection, did I realize I rather listlessly floated through those days. There were times I fooled myself into believing I had experienced serene moments, or moments of feature-film-like profundity. "I'm getting it," I thought. "I have it together, and I am living a decent life." Or the more obnoxious and fatuous esteem-booster, "I'm on my way." Well all right, then! Let's raise a glass to that, shall we? Are we not *all* "on our way"? (Yes, indeed. With will and determination, along with a good gut hunch, we will be on our way to that there yonder star.)

Very few ever really fully *arrive*. (I'm restraining myself from the tempting "life is a journey" adage. I'm keeping it on ice for now.) Even as we "get it" we continuously strive for further understanding. Life is absurd and existence really can be stranger than fiction. It is in this light that we traverse the darkness and potholes of life. Writers can always be better. Guitarists can always achieve better command and compose sweeter licks. Likewise for individuals just living their lives. The six-minute abs version of life

– along with the go-to sitcom-style, aphoristic one-liners – doesn't track reality. The important thing to realize is once we start to understand how and why to remain engaged in life, it becomes a fun and meaningful struggle. Without this type of struggle, life would be discouraging and unfortunate. And worse still, many people do not even realize they exist in this vacuum of indifference and emotional (and intellectual) dilapidation. I can't decide which is worse: knowing and not caring about our carelessness, or simply being blind to it. Once we start to care about really living, we start to notice that the struggle is constantly paying dividends. Sometimes we smile, and sometimes we cry. It is sometimes the best of times, and sometimes the worst. Understanding, though, how to think and approach these feelings gives us a sense of insuperable confidence to continue this ride. We only get a few decades, so it makes little sense not to do the best we can.

I am not unaware of the vertiginous effects of spinning in place. Your voice is loud and clear. I still carry and bear the mark of vestigial whiplash. Reflecting on one's own apathy can be a bit numbing. But seeing and understanding the struggle, Dear Reader – the uphill struggle – is what makes a patently absurd life ultimately worthwhile. French existentialist philosopher, Albert Camus, was famous for his idea of the "Absurd" and his solution to the concomitant dilemma. That life is absurd is a given. We humans are meaning-mongers, and we live in a world that provides no extrinsic "meaning." We need it. We look for it. The world does not provide it – at least not in the immaculately packaged, store brand version that "self-help" books would have us perceive. So, "we" together with – and living in - the "world," provide a rich and unalterable recipe for absurdity. Camus's solution was to embrace it as is, and provide our own meaning (more on this later). We must continue to do the often-inglorious work of "figuring it out." And even with our iron wills and determinations this will be a difficult task. It is a task that will sometimes fail. Failure, though, is not the end of the road. Life empowerment books – which, I have to grudgingly admit, vaguely categorizes my own work – also speak to you about picking up and dusting yourself off. The difference is they are usually referring to a particular activity or event ("go get that job!"), and not about simply living - or at least not *truly* living. In other words, I'm saying the details are not as important if you can take a step back and look at the bigger decision making principles at work. As I mentioned earlier, "You can do it!" isn't quite cutting it. I will stop talking about me, lest I provide you with an unwanted autobiography. Allow me just to make one more observation.

Attending a private school has its perks. My middle and high school was a college prep boarding school, and the environment was two parts stifling and one part oddly freeing. Interesting, but true. My formative years were forged on an enlightened intellectual freedom. The administration simultaneously ran a tight ship and gave you plenty of cerebral pasture to roam. I wasn't much of an intellectual scavenger. I wasn't much of an emotional detective either. I did, in these years, develop a passion for arts. I developed a passion for passionate things. (I began learning the guitar and playing music among other things.) This passion, although at times severely misguiding me throughout the years, did help set the stage for my engagement in bigger things. I cared enough to take a closer look at my surroundings and circumstances. I remember, though, sitting in that strangely oppressive interview – my first time in tie and jacket (at thirteen squeaky years) – where the admissions committee quizzed me on why I thought I should be allowed through the gates. My dad had told me what to say had they asked certain questions (so I could be accepted – a smart move in retrospect). The whole business felt sordid and slimy. I figured, "I should know what to say, here." From then on, having an answer for myself always had an enduring appeal. Being told what to do and say is bad enough. However, there is something worse - being told what to *think* has to be the most authoritarian and dictatorial of infractions. Sometimes we have to do and say certain things (for our own good, or not), but being able to *think* about them in an engaged, and intellectually honest, manner should be the pinnacle of our concern. Anyone can do this, I'm happy to say. I'm glad this college-oriented boarding school ultimately allowed for this simple but important measure.

In summation: you don't have to be professor curled lip to think about and enjoy life. You may find that you enjoy assuming this role – and that is fine too. I enjoy discussing the hard stuff, and the university stuff. I enjoy Socrates, Hume, and Russell (some will appreciate the name-dropping). It thrills me to tread the almost unnavigable ocean of esotericism. It is not necessary for anyone else to do this. You do not have to hold degrees or have a great job or own a lot of stuff (I don't). We are all really Joe Blows anyway, as we all put our pants on one leg at a time. (I think Einstein, however, must surely have had custom made, single leg pantaloons.) Forget the unwaveringly British, ruler wielding, professor curled lip. We don't need him to move forward. Being in control of our thoughts and reactions is the only thing we need to be aware of to start. And it is in this consideration that we now turn to chapter two.

CH. 2 BEING IN CONTROL

Afoot and lighthearted I take to the open road
Healthy, free, the world before me,
The long brown path before me leading
me wherever I choose.
Henceforth I ask not good fortune.
Henceforth I whimper no more, postpone
no more, need nothing,
Done with indoor complaints, libraries,
querulous criticisms,
Strong and content I travel the open road
– Walt Whitman *Song of the Open Road*

The American-led literature as well as lifestyle movement, Transcendentalism, is an interesting movement in one notable way. This is, in my opinion, its ability to be both transcendent and stubbornly irksome. The most notable authors of this movement – Emerson, Thoreau, and Whitman – display moments of unyielding beauty, simplicity, and sagacity. These men also manage to put in ink some of the most abstruse, turgid, and unfriendly prose and poetry ever coined. The philosophy can also tend to be a bit saccharine in its idealism. It's a vexatious case of wanting to love them (certainly feeling kinship to the movement of natural simplicity), but not always being able to do so. Though the above example from Whitman is one of the simplest, purest forms of timeless emotional allure. His ability to express with such stark, rich imagery the invigorating idea of "leaving it behind" is fascinating. The open road and the open mind, denuded of all unimportant blandishments and superfluities (although I might not reject a library), seems a place of undeniable comfort. Tacit of course is that typical "indoor comforts" are not all that great, and that what one should truly crave is the life of being happy where one is and with what one has. I glean from the poem more than just a nod to wanderlust and rejection of materialism; there also appears to be something else glimmering beneath the surface – that an accessibility or effortlessness should pervade our self-control. We can, with little recourse to material or even "civilized" help, understand our place in the cosmos and control our "destiny" under any circumstances. There is something to this. This may be a stretched interpretation of a one-note theme, but there is something to be said for retaining control, patience, and understanding amidst life's onslaught of chaotic madness.

We might wonder whether Whitman would condone contemporary remedies for this madness (which has become much worse). Today, one sees everywhere the clichéd slogans and general platitudes of self-determination, as well as various anti-defeatist tautologies. These are surely motivating in some respect. It has always been the case that one needs a general level of self-confidence to pull oneself up by the bootstraps. Muttering something like, "times are tough," isn't enough; we are born into a losing struggle that ends the same for everyone, priest and peasant. So it is no far stretch (for the need) to assume the roll of defiant, stoic, and self-determined leader, an unwavering captain of oneself, one possessing the confidence to defy all odds and ultimately prevail.

This, upon first glance, is not only a healthy attitude, but also even a necessary attitude, if one wishes to slog through the vagaries of life. However, one can take this idea decidedly too far. I believe there is a marked transition between a reasonable level of self-determination, and a reasonable level of the rational acceptance of events. The notion of *too much* self-determination is a real thing, and this is rarely argued.

You never really have to tell anyone about the positive attributes of moderation. Most individuals will attest to this Aristotelian maxim. The "Goldie-Locks" position is lauded and is certainly secured in the minds of most rational people. However, not all things are amenable to a particular degree of moderation (a claim with which I agree), but I strongly believe that self-determination – and, in the case of self-congratulation, even more so – that moderation is invariably necessary.

Moderation may be somewhat of a misnomer. I'm not arguing for moderation's sake alone. (I never argue for the "sake" of "sake.") But, rather, I argue that too much self-determination holds dangerous implications (as well as ideological connotations). I mentioned earlier that we see a constant influx of pithy formulations concerning self-determination. Some are about not giving up, others about never letting situational circumstances deter your unyielding mindset, and so on. The intrinsic problem here lies with the inviolable outcome of defeat. You will be defeated at times, and this is certain. You must certainly dust yourself off and continue. But what will your mindset then be? Are you jumping back on the same horse, or will you hop on a new horse adorning yourself with new armor? How many times will one venture fail before you accept reality? For the sake of maintaining a healthy relationship with your self (and consequently, with others), the realization of possible defeat – true defeat – has to become internalized.

Whether we realize it or not, a sort of superstitious self-confidence pervades many of our lives, and this becomes the basis of much consternation. I've noticed that contriving a celestial sense of purpose often gives many the misguided sense they are "destined for glory," or "won't fail." I also have often heard the utterly inane phrase, "I can't fail." You most assuredly can - indeed will - fail. This is not debatable. Most individuals uttering these phrases are doing so with an innocuous sense of self-confidence; but this really isn't so innocuous. If you believe that you have it written in the stars for you to succeed – or, better yet, because you simply "want it bad enough" – and that all plans will come to fruition, the deeper the infliction of pain will be come the inevitable failure. Now, this isn't to say that one will always fail at every endeavor; that is also an absurd proposition. But it is to point out that a "gut feeling" is far from substantiating an unflinching confidence.

You may have witnessed certain persons spiraling into an ill-gotten depression simply on account of not succeeding at something in which they felt there was no possible room for failure. Imagine, if you are able, the woman not getting the job for which she worked so hard (naturally peppered with a bit of desultory prayer for good measure). Consider the kid who studied for hours and days on end to get accepted to a college, and for what? No acceptance was forthcoming. If we can expect that things won't always (or even often) work out for us – no matter how wholehearted the gut hunch – the painful questions "why me?" or "why now?" will not be quite so devastating. This is unnecessary, and it causes unnecessary emotional damage. What is the solution?

The solution to this problem should be very simple. We have to come to terms with the forces of reality, with the ineluctable vicissitudes of life. This may sound cruel and unpleasant, but tough dice. The universe doesn't care to cater to us. (Doesn't have the ability to care at all, I should say.) Being confident enough to control your self in a whirlwind of uncertainty is the key to ultimate happiness. In other words, you will become happiest when you realize you will not always be happy – indeed, that you sometimes will be miserable. The irony is that the misery is almost always induced by the fact you did not think you could be miserable! Accepting reality – as I will constantly advocate and reiterate – is the ultimate key to prosperity. One can learn what one can and cannot realistically do or perform by assessing the real constituents of each endeavor. Will you then still be unhappy? Sure, sometimes you will. Will you still falsely assess certain goals and abilities? This is certainly the case. But this is the road we travel, and acceptance is paramount. Learning to be comfortable with uncertainty is vital for a healthy, emotional state of mind.

We can reasonably reach the conclusion that self-determination is absolutely necessary in a world where the stars aren't aligning or misaligning in our favor; or in a world where our "gut feeling" is any more predicting than a crystal ball or set of tarot cards. However, with this new frame of mind, we will learn to pick up the pieces of our (if only momentarily) shattered lives. Hopefully each time the amount of pieces will diminish, and hopefully each time we will accrue less and less damage from failure. We will be accustomed to a life of uncertainty. This life of accepting uncertainty will open doors and windows to unforeseen vistas of opportunity, as well as present beautiful new challenges. One horse gallops away and another emerges for a new journey – it may not be a big journey, but it will always be one at least worth investigating. Let us not be so myopic and solipsistic in our vision. We can open our periphery and accept new visions of defeat and opportunity.

This answers big existential questions. If I may be allowed a cliché of my own, here: In artistic terms, you can be cognitively and emotionally available to start painting the canvas with a preexisting idea, but when this idea goes awry you can simply transition into what your error has then given you. You can figuratively *become* the canvas. You can then assert control at all times.

Controlling our emotions and reactions to the pervasive lack of control in life is something with which Whitman would have probably agreed. He, like Thoreau or Muir, may have felt the need to move into the wild or hit the open road. This is, I think, a partial copout. My immediate emotional reaction is to agree with these literary figures, these giants of simple wisdom. Being in control, however, undoubtedly means accepting *whatever* society may provide us, and that also means not always being able to abscond from reality into a bucolic utopia. Whitman's open road is a glorious paean to the poetic vagabond in all of us. Joni Mitchell verbalizes the dichotomy of these two polar existences as she opines about her album *Hejira*: "The whole 'Hejira' album was really inspired... I wrote the album while traveling cross-country by myself and there is this restless feeling throughout it... The sweet loneliness of solitary travel." This would show that Whitman and Thoreau almost had it right. Controlling ourselves, though, comes in the form a tough pill. We cannot always abdicate the throne of personal responsibility and societal expectations. If we can recognize this fact, then an open road or emotional pilgrimage can take place wherever we might be.

Some, however, believe that any or all of these circumstances are part of some plan. "At any rate," they might insist, "everything happens for a reason." Let us see if this idea holds water. Read on.

Ch. 3 "EVERYTHING HAPPENS FOR A REASON"

> Never allow yourself to be too impressed about a belief's popularity. Reality is not determined by a majority vote.
> – Guy P. Harrison

I'm actually blown away by the sheer intransigence and staying power of this phrase. It is an idea that seems to be imperishable. It is yet another cliché that has been sloganized, beaten into our cultural and emotional subconscious, and is one that has a remarkable ubiquity. You unsurprisingly hear this around every corner and under every conceivable set of conditions. One has to internalize the slogan for it to have any considerable effect. By this I don't mean actually contemplating its merits. One just needs to have adopted this phrase into their lexicon (and develop the requisite phraseology). Hearing it repeated *ad nauseam* or being inculcated with the idea (again, typically by being bludgeoned into submission with an unreflective and philistine repetition) will usually do the trick. Thinking about it – and not about oneself – for longer than a few moments renders the concept unintelligible. If it then is at all intelligible it still suffers in light of its morally bankrupt condition. It is philosophically inert – a nullity.

A colloquial example can be given. I was in Walgreens one day loitering in the "card" isle thinking to myself, "Jesus, am I turning into the wide-eyed, edgy maladroit who struggles indecisively about which birthday card to purchase?" (This apparently is the case.) While conversing with myself, half consumed in buyer anxiety (they only turn thirty-eight once, for Christ sake), I happened upon two women discussing personal problems (ok, so they happened upon me and I unapologetically and professionally eavesdropped). One blabbered on about an annoying array of "issues" over which she was clearly struggling. The other stood nodding, seemingly engaged, and provided a friendly ear. (Men, alternatively, tend to provide instead a friendly beer. "Those problems *are* interesting! How 'bout a brew for your troubles? The ballgame is over and I have to buy a birthday card before dinner.")

So, anyway, the one rehashing her problems and concerns finishes by weighing her potential options: "So, I may go back to school to be an X-Ray tech...everything happens for a reason, ya know?" I'm certain my eyes widened in both alarm and disbelief. Did I just hear that? Let us take a few moments to disentangle all that is odd about that comment.

Evidently, as the woman would have it, her decision to go back to school (or not) to be an X-Ray technician (or not) is something that has already been decided (pre-ordained?) *Who* is deciding or orchestrating this, or *why* it is this way are questions I will address shortly. Consider just *how* this is done. If we are presupposing that any possibility not only *can be* but also *is* "for" a reason, then we have already considered the impossible. For how is it possible that *any* possible future outcome is decided in advance? There is an infinite list of possible scenarios. They cannot all logically occur or be allowed to occur. If attending school is *supposed* to happen, then *not* attending school was not supposed to. That's it. A set outcome cannot simply run around willy-nilly, choosing its final place of rest. People change their minds all the time. Let us say that the woman decides not to go back to school. That then would be what was *supposed* to happen.

So what, then, of her school plans? Were they or were they not, in fact, part of the "plan"? She might argue that oscillation in her decision-making process is of no consequence. This essentially is what is being said: "had I went back to school, that would have happened for a reason; if I did not go back then *that* would have happened for a reason." This is sly, and it is having it both ways. The problem is she is already assuming what she is trying to prove. How could any possible scenario *not* be the "right" one when all one has to do is *wait to see what actually happens?* How easy is it to post date or post scribe an event? *X* happened so *x* happened for a reason. Well, *of course* that can be asserted! It cannot, however, be vouched for. What if she shaved her head, moved to Utah, and married a Mormon? Everything happens for a reason. What if she joined a Congolese tribe living in the jungles of central Africa and practiced a form of witchcraft-like animism? Everything happens for a reason. Became a deranged killer? Oh, sweet serendipity – how you know me like a book. It was meant to be. Decides that she no longer believes that everything happens for a reason? You got it: Everything…Well, you get the picture.

(I found my card and quickly moved on. I got home and successfully delivered my card before dinner. Sweet felicity, everything *does* happen for a reason.)

Shall we take a closer look at this phenomenon? Usually (but not always) originating and branching from some form of religion (or something very much like it), the phrase "*everything happens for a reason*" has surely been the zeitgeist of almost every age. (What else can we do to cull some form of control in an absurd world where there is very little?) The very notion of American Exceptionalism ("city on a hill") is inexorably tied to this sense of providential guidance. Some*one* or some*thing* is looking out for number one. I have God on *my side* (said almost everyone ever involved in a war). This was an unexpectedly bad turn, but all will "turn out" – everything happens for a reason. These are things one hears almost on a daily basis. It is tough to conceptualize being the author of your actions *all* the time, through good and bad, easy and rough. But there it is. (Later in the book we will see there is another potential problem with this idea.) I will attempt now to point out a few philosophical flaws and inconsistencies with our idea.

One of the salient reasons for including this chapter is the disheartening amount of times this illogical and philistine (and morally slippery) phrase is being wantonly spat out. In the wake of natural disasters (for a heavily documented instance) I consistently hear statements such as, "God was looking out for me, so we made it through the storm," or "Thank God we made it ok." Well, I dare inquire, what about those who didn't *make it ok?* Perhaps they didn't propitiate a deity – or the right deity (there *are* so many from which to choose) – or maybe they never had some*one* or some*thing* to look over them. But what if they did putatively have the very same teleological and providential outlook as the survivors? This is certainly the case much of the time. *X* and *Y* were both Christians, say (or Muslims or New Age hipsters), but *X* managed to survive and *Y* did not. What could possibly be the cosmic *cause* of this? By what measure does God (or the universe or whatever) discriminate on whom or what does or does not get wiped out? Is there some sort of methodical system? Checks and balances? Celestial bop-a-mole? Supreme fiat, or maybe just boredom? Perhaps *Y* didn't pray or wish (or accept good tidings from the universe) as hard or as much as *X*?

Furthermore, why would such a providential entity discriminate against or be choosy about *anyone?* What's the point? Why "watch over" anyone at all, for that matter? In the Christian sense, things become even muddier. For instance, why would an all-knowing, all-loving God let *anyone* die in such a cruel and pitiless manner - natural disasters, terminal illness, starvation, etc.? One can posit that God did not *cause* such things, but this God certainly can *stop* these things can He not? Your options: God has the power to stop atrocities, but chooses not to – in which case he is evil (and not just mercurial…imagine how you would use this power if you possessed it); God wants to stop these atrocities but *cannot* – in which case he is not omnipotent, and therefore no god for the record books. God both knows the future and chooses to do nothing, *or* he does not know anything of future happenstance (which, we can fairly say, does not make one omniscient). These options do not so far bode well for the deterministic crowd.

I know the typical response, and it is another massive piece of illogic. "Well, I'm not sure why *others* had to die. We cannot know God's plan. It's a mystery (and just might forever remain so. Who knows? I lived though, and I have a potluck dinner tonight. If you will excuse me from this scathing interrogation…)" Part of this always makes me slightly nauseous every time I hear it. The very idea that people have to (ostensibly) needlessly die and suffer for some sort of mysterious plan to be optimally wrought makes me quiver with disgust. This is how some rationalize pain and suffering; there is a cosmic plan, but we just don't know what it is. What omniscient god-like entity (who in some cases is all-loving, lest we forget) cannot bring into light a plan or prove a point without needless suffering and misery and annihilation? If tornados and tsunamis and volcanoes and *natural selection* (!) need to exist at all, why not just save everyone from the looming catastrophes? Why are some saved and not others?

The next sentence is important, and I address the ones who boldly declaim such unconscionable things. *It is either a mystery or it is not.* You choose. God either willingly threw forth a divine hand to protect your life – in which case He also *willingly* let others perish – or it is a mystery why they died *and also why* you lived. It cannot logically be both. You cannot have all the glory, I'm sorry to say. You also cannot have this type of obscene foresight, because you do not possess mental powers that the next average human being does not possess. And who are we fragile things all but mere mammals? (Remember *that* next time you wish to chime in about humility.)

(The same concept is applicable to all forms of "everything happens for a reason," including but not limited to: *my dog lived, I got the job, grandma's surgery went well, and we made it to the volleyball nationals* [along with other comparable forms of mundane piffle.] Someone's dog did not live, someone remains unemployed, someone's grandma had complications, and some poor, athletically challenged team was rebuffed for its efforts. So much the worse for *them*.)

Let us not also forget that the inclusive phrase heading our chapter is necessarily fatalistic. There is no need to pray or propitiate if everything happens for a reason. Indeed, we can jump off of buildings, we can drive with our eyes closed, and we can walk straight up to a hungry bear. None of those things matter, because whatever takes place is supposed to do so. And your continued existence *or* death is already duly decided. This, you'll notice, doesn't prevent the supplicants and the devout from taking a quick and selfish knee. Can we all now admit the stupidity of such a notion? I hope so.

There is one more important idea that needs to be included. It is about existence and essence. I'll just make short shrift for now. The bottom line is this: you make yourself. You make and guide yourself through your life. It's very simple. You are the author of your own actions. This will need some clarification. Everyone and everything around you – your reality – has some form of affect on you and your actions. This is a form of causation. Causality is apparent and consistent with everything we know about the world, physics, and the state of the brain. Many people do not realize what is going on upstairs in the locked down compartments of our mechanical brains. You, Dear Reader, have no "I" that is somehow separate from your mechanistic brain activity. This is what modern neuroscience tells us, and it makes hash of the timeworn, classic idea of free will (which would *still* need to be explained in the deterministic universe where everything happens for a reason). Free will is illusory, and we are slaves to our neurobiology and to causality. If any and every thing is determined and happens for a reason, then I curiously ask: where is the fee will in that? Free will seems to fall flat no matter the confines of our discussion. (Having the Boss hand down or prescribe free will is also a bit of lost irony on the devout.)

This is purely scientific, though, and does not affect the way we feel. We see this a lot. For instance, the universe doesn't have a "point" or "meaning." The mindless replication of DNA is "unthinking," but we obviously think anyway. Recall my mention of Albert Camus and his idea of the Absurd. A species like us – the only one so far capable of such reflection – is continuously coming to terms with living in a world that provides no external reflection. In his view, we have three possible solutions for dealing with this absurdity. We can commit suicide and end it – the easy and cheap way out. We can develop some format, scenario, or storyline to equip us with a meaning we can use – such as religion. Lastly, we can simply accept these terms and do the best with what we have. We can create our own story and our own meaning. (This is admittedly a perfunctory look at Camus' work, and I suggest reading his work directly.) So, we humans created and fostered culture(s), and we continue to recreate ourselves and revivify our lives. We, and our creations, evolve in every respect. I will try to break down why we do this, and what it means for us.

A quick point about myself: I am an existentialist[1]. I also adhere to logical positivism in some respect. (This is a school adhering to strict rules of language and definitions. This school typically adheres to the idea that we only have one being, and that being is only a material one. This is known as *physicalism* or *ontological monism* – setting it apart from mind/body dualists. The later relativists, along with the Rortyean post-philosophical school, also adhere to an ontological monism.) For those of you philosophically inclined, you will be quick to point out these platforms can be somewhat antagonistic of each other. But much to the comic avail of existentialism, I can afford to practice some parts of almost all philosophical disciplines. I create myself. I can choose to develop different trains of thought, ethical platforms, and lifestyles from different philosophical traditions... and change them if I want. I am not a strict disciple of Plato, Aristotle, or Aquinas, Descartes, Locke, or Hume, Kant, Kierkegaard, or Sartre, or Russell, but I can develop a workable aggregate of ideas

---

[1] A quick note on this may be necessary. I do not know how many academicians or *philosophes* would be deconstructing my claim to existentialism. It's possible that "true" existentialists may balk at this arrogation of identification, especially since I go on to discuss determinism and the lack of "free will." This, according to Isaiah Berlin – who believes existentialism to be a sort of emotional child or offshoot of Romanticism – a movement that notoriously rejected "otherness" and harmony, but instead rather rejoiced in the will to power and the rejection of Enlightenment values – is one of the main problems of existentialism. I both agree and disagree. If it isn't appropriate to give myself the title I will concede the point. It's not an important battle for me to fight. But I do identify with much of existential thought and ideal – even as it seems irreconcilable with science or moral value. Sartre noted adamantly that existentialism was indeed humanism, and with this I agree. (To the casual reader: so sorry for this excursion into academia.)

that I find appealing. I have my qualms with all of these giants, but I have an immense respect for all of them. That particular point is apropos of existentialism in practice.

"This is interesting, but rather bleak and boring," you may say. It might initially seem this way, but it is not really so. Why is that? The hard facts are just that. We do not live our lives for the indifferent, meaningless cosmos. We live *our* lives. What does it mean to ask of some "ultimate meaning" of the universe? How can rocks and gas have meaning for you? (Shout out to my cosmology and astronomy friends in the room.) Likewise, what does it mean to ask what *your special purpose* is? You have just *one* special purpose? A logical positivist would dismiss metaphysical ontology as meaningless. (That just means they find the idea of abstract being – being more than what you physically are - a bit silly). It does not mean anything to have a presupposed "purpose." I don't believe or disbelieve in something based on whether or not I *like* it. Or whether not I *feel* it. Also, as an existentialist, I realize I can form my own essence. Existentialism champions personal responsibility and reality. We make our own choices. We reap our own consequences. We don't have to thank anyone for our successes (unless they are directly attributable to someone, and then it would be polite), and we need not blame anyone for our faults or defeats. (This doesn't mean we cannot or should not be sympathetic to others. That is an entirely different point.) We don't have a particular essence. We simply *exist*. Life, as Camus starkly puts it, is patently absurd. It is also beautiful. We can embrace the absurdity or pointlessness of it, and relish the beauty. We can create beauty of our own. Leading French existentialist, Jean Paul Sartre, wrote of a plastic knife analogy. Here, Sartre says, we are not put here for a particular purpose like a plastic knife. A plastic knife is created for a specific purpose. We, however, are like a stone sitting in the forest: we could be used as a cutting implement, but it would be rather by chance. We can serve many purposes or, quite simply, none at all. We are perennially defined by everything *and* nothing. We are not only fathers, wives, children, office employees, Republicans, whites, blacks, gays, Christians, comedians, nerds, athletes and so on – we are all of these things. We *consistently evolve and change our minds.* This is what it means to be human. We cannot rise above or opt out of the vicissitudes of the human experience. We exist and therefore we are all exposed to everything life throws at us. What we do makes us who we are. There is simply no "I'm *meant* to do this" or "everything happens for a reason" or "it has to get better soon." These are alignments with fantasy, not with reality. We are a collection of biologically and chemically evolved organs, including a magnificent brain. We are blueprints (a slightly inappropriate term) of DNA instruction. We are also musicians, poets, scientists, martial artists, dads, husbands, mothers, sisters, and lovers of history and cinema and on and on. We may not always be one or any of these things, but we have no charted essence. We just exist. In a popular song from the rock band, Incubus, singer Brandon Boyd forcefully and passionately suggests, "Why not try to make yourself?" It appears to be a perfectly reasonable question and suggestion.

So what does all this mean? The bigger picture is that there is no bigger picture. You and me and every individual of the world makes that picture what it is. As one timeless and insightful axiom has it: shit happens. Pointless, heartbreaking and inevitable stuff (in the statistical sense, not the deterministic one) happens all too frequently. We can work together to synthesize a lucid understanding about reality. We can stop considering ourselves so special, and learn we are no better "looked out for" than anyone else. It makes it much easier in starting a compassionate understanding and conversation of our human condition when

we embrace these facts. It is a jumping off point. We square
back to first base, we understand our position as existing with
no particular essence (a *tabula rasa*), and we can communicate
with each other with much less division or derision. By speaking
rationally and fairly we can understand and care for one another.
I think politics would improve (don't expect too much on that
front), religious sectarianism would become diminished, and our
understanding of where we fit in respect to others would make
us doubly compassionate and considerate. Once we understand
that we are basically like everybody else in this grand sense, we
can care more efficiently for everybody. In this sense, then, our
awareness can lead to a more astute and tender engagement in
life. That is enough purpose for me. When you consider it in that
light, a narcissistic view of a particular interest - X-Ray education,
say – seems pallid. (I privately wished a hearty good luck to my
fellow Walgreens shopper. She was just trying to make the best
of her circumstances. We can all understand and appreciate that.)

Being observant of our language is a way to understand what
we want – and can get – out of life. It also, as is the case in this
chapter, can help us differentiate sense and nonsense. If we can
navigate through life with this ability, then we would save a
lot of time, energy, and fretting. Chapter four provides another
important and specific example of this.

Ch. 4 PLAYING WITH LANGUAGE

> But if thought corrupts language, language
> can also corrupt thought.
> – George Orwell

The above quotation is taken from Orwell's essay, "Politics and the English Language." In this essay, Orwell excoriates the panoply of bad writing devices currently in use. (Well, this was written in 1946; Orwell today is probably rolling in his grave.) He condemns "dying metaphors," "operators," and what he refers to as "meaningless words." I only partially agree with Orwell's assessment on some of these devices. Maybe that is because I fall into a couple of his categories. It is clear, though, that we must pay attention to what we say. As evidenced in the last chapter, not considering the implications of an "everyday" phrase could – and almost always does – affect our thought processes. This gets us into trouble, and leads us ultimately to disengage from a meaningful life. If we disengage from our language and definitions – that is, if we do not pay attention to what we say and what we mean – life can become muddled and disorderly. If, like I say in my subtitle, becoming engaged in life can lead to a happier existence, then becoming engaged in what we say and mean will make us happier as well. Many of us go through life dodging emotional or intellectual bullets because we simply do not care to focus on the words leaving our mouths. Words have meanings, and that fact really matters. I spend much of this chapter focusing on a particularly egregious example: the difference between knowing and believing.

Many people conflate the terms knowing and believing. They use the term "know" when they should use the term "believe." What does this mean, and why does it even matter? We can only know facts or, as the Carl Sagan conception has it, get as close to them as scientifically possible. We can certainly believe very strongly, but that should not be confused with *knowing* something. If we can provide evidence and corroboration for some fact, then we can claim to know that thing (insofar as "knowing" it is possible: philosophical metaphysics, in my opinion, is a dead avenue for this topic, and philosophy of mind – in the scientific paradigm – should partition our theory of knowledge. Carl Sagan's conception of truth, in scientific terms, is always getting nearer and nearer, but never quite "reaching," the truth). Truth is objective, but believing is *sub*jective and stands irrespective of the facts. Beliefs could be true or false, and this is really beside the point. We need to understand what we mean when we say such things. This difference can be critical.

How many times have you heard or said something similar to this: "I believe it to be true" or "I just *feel* it is true"? These and kindred statements are uttered on an almost hourly basis. It's very normal, and no one really thinks anything of it. But there is a problem with those statements and those "feelings." It is simply that they are not true. Well, they *might* be true, but there is no de facto connection. Work has to be involved. You cannot simply wish something to be true. I have to explain that statement as well, because the common contention is that truth apparently is also subjective. The feelings are subjective and then, apparently, so is the truth. The truth, almost as if by transitive property, is subjective simply because the *feelings* are subjective. I'm not sure how one gleans subjectivity in truth from that proposition. Feelings are altogether different from knowledge of factual matters. Nevertheless, the truth *is* actually objective – often times demonstrably so (to the utter indifference of the "subjective feelings" promulgators). I take the next few paragraphs to break down and explain this more clearly. (Pragmatist philosophers, like Richard Rorty, take the approach to science developed by Thomas Kuhn, where there is thought to be no actual "truth," and that our knowledge just moves in paradigm shifts. In other words, there is no real way that you could know if you discovered the "truth" even if you did, in fact, stumble upon it. They say we have been wrong in the past, so we will be wrong in the future. According to Rorty, we only have strong justifications for beliefs. This line of thinking seems to me to be a bait and switch, or another simple linguistic issue. The Sagan approach to truth makes perfect sense, and we can certainly feel comfortable calling something the truth with the proper evidence – even if that thing later shifts with new or further evidence[2].)

Some folks will then nervously or pushily ask, "don't my feelings count?" Yes. Your subjective experience counts. Your feelings, along with those of almost everyone else, do indeed count and are also important. In fact, I can think of nothing more foundational, decisive, and essential than subjective experience. I wouldn't even be able to properly define "objective experience" – the phrase is somewhat nonsensical. (How does one experience

---

[2] Think Newtonian physics "supplanted" by Einsteinian physics, and then that later conflicting with quantum mechanics. All of these things are still true according to the evidence – as opposed to, say, a Ptolemaic (geocentric) view of the solar system, which was never true, although many believed it to be so.

something objectively? Experience, really by definition, connotes subjectivity. Again – we could be as "right" with our experiences as it gets, but that would just be incidental.) The key is to understand that truth is *objective*, and that it stands irrespective and unwaveringly in the face of subjective experience.

Of course, finding the truth of a certain proposition usually *starts* with some subjective experience. We experience something – curiosity, confusion – and we develop a hypothesis for solving a dilemma or answering a question. This is the *modus operandi* of science. Ultimately, scientific facts - or truths - are not constrained by the initial subjective experience. The truth, and facts, lay in a plane of untouchable objectivity. Science can overturn its previous findings, but it does so by way of methodological processes and peer reviewed corroboration…not on a gut hunch. (I think Rorty focuses too much on some Platonic, philosophical conception of Truth, and loses sight of the *method* of obtaining corroborated and well-situated information. I'm sure if he were here he would argue me into a hole about it…and probably win.) In summation of this point: experiences do matter but *truth* is playing by a set of inviolable rules. The truth is there whether we find it or not; it also stands whether we *like* it or not. To employ a banal truism: it is what it is.

Some of the pseudo-philosophically inclined would argue that *facts* and *truths* are somehow separate entities. These individuals contend that just because a scientific fact is universally accepted, it does not then make this fact suddenly *true* – as if *truth* is something conceivably different. This "argument" is a non-argument, and a foolish bit of wordplay and semantics tweaking. Presumably, these individuals hold truth to be some Platonic thing on some Platonic "higher plane." Listen, folks. Words have to mean something. In this case, simply asserting an inequity between truth and fact is itself a definitional absurdity. How are they defining truth, then?

There is no baseline proposition for this assertion that isn't hinged on more undefined (and probably indefinable) terms. What does that mean? It means if someone invokes a higher power (or something else) as the *truth* - this happens incessantly - and states that scientific facts are just illusions, then this person has merely postulated that a higher power exists in the very first place. That is one step further removed from where we started with scientific facts. So what, then? They just add more (mind bending) work and more terms to have to define. How is that clarifying anything, exactly? Using fanciful "woo" language does not trump workable and testable definitions and propositions. After all, scientists are not simply asserting that gravity is a fact or that it is true. They test and test, and then test some more. The arrogance in doing anything else is barely tolerable. Standing on a foundation of cement is always safer than standing on water – no matter how authoritatively, smarmily, or condescendingly you state that your water is something else. It is just water.

People often state they "know" something when what they really mean is they "believe" something. This usually occurs innocuously and unsuspectingly. They typically don't mind if you correct them on the difference. No big deal, right? Well, for a particular incident it is not a big deal. When we look at it as a critical way of thinking it becomes more important. I will return to that point shortly. *"I know there are ghosts,"* they might say. They may follow that with, *"I've seen one."* But did they see one? This is where a subjective experience often falls flat. Can we trust our experiences? Many times we cannot. We can trust that we *had* an experience - but what does that even mean? We know from many fMRI scans and neuroscience studies that we - our consciousness - miss something like three-fourths of what is actually happening in the recesses of our brains. We know that we constantly misremember, and even sometimes completely fabricate certain events. We also know that we constantly see patterns and agents where there are none. We all do this, but it is a bit more vivid with conspiracy theorists (one frequently sees political commentators and doomsday "preppers," to name a few, develop extreme paranoia about things that are not actually happening or even likely to occur). Conspiracy theorists throw rational thinking directly out the window. They are concerned less about facts and more about what *they* (subjective alert!) consider to be factual. In one case, I knew a woman who said that instead of paranoia she suffered from "*truth*anoia." On vivid display is the contention that if you wish it hard enough any information can become "truth." This is when people become dangerous.

Making connections where none exist is not a surprising trend to find. Seeing patterns and agents is an evolutionary byproduct. Mistaking the wind rustling through the grass for a deadly lion is the reason our ancestors survived. It is an inherited trait. The ones who always assumed it was wind in the grass are no longer here to make their genetic presence felt. The lion gobbled them up. So, it is not surprising to learn that this is the kind of animal we are[3]. People certainly have specific experiences - and nobody would deny them that - but what those experiences actually are, and what they actually mean (if anything), is an entirely different animal.

Individuals will assign a specific meaning to a particular event or experience. Yet, another individual will assign a completely different meaning to the *same* event or experience. Subjective experiences are not the criteria by which to judge what is *actually true*. The facts are not voted on by plebiscite, and here democratic appeal has no luster. Seeing an angel, feeling a presence, near death or out-of-body experiences are all circumstances that so far make sense under a scientific light – and they fall soundly within

---

[3] See Michael Shermer for well-written details on this subject.

the purview of science. Neuroscience is blazing a trail where once biology and Newtonian physics blazed a trail – deconstructing the credulous darkness one test at a time. Science always one-ups itself, and it always emerges the victor in the game of "we don't have the answers, so it will remain a mystery." Each time, once strongly held mythological beliefs are knocked down to the natural levels of explanation. Much of what was once mysterious (or maybe considered "supernatural") is now explicable through naturalistic methods. What remains in any degree opaque will one day be elucidated by the same methods. The champions of the supernatural or mystical are seen grasping at the ever-diminishing straw that is being sucked out the window of incredulity. This window should not be frightening. This idea should be welcomed with waiting arms. Now we can discover the *real* meanings to the mysterious. That is a much more exciting and rewarding case of playing detective. Here is a short quiz:

A.) That is evocative and mysterious. It will forever remain so.
B.) That is evocative and mysterious. I can tell you immediately what it is – it is supernatural in origin (gods, ghosts, bigfoots, pearly white lights, UFO)
C.) That is evocative and mysterious. I hope to dig deeper to find what is really going on. Reality is beautiful.

I should have worked for more C's growing up. A's and B's are overrated.

Cognitive bias and cognitive dissonance play an important part in our dangerous language game. "So let me get this straight. You were thinking about him, the phone rang, you picked up, and lo and behold it was he on the line? Get out of town!! So this must happen a lot, right? What a crazy, telepathic, zoned-into-the-universe-energy-waves-chi you must have!" Well, now that we put pen to paper we see that this almost never happens. The fourteen million times we are thinking about our friends and they *don't* call are conveniently forgotten. It only takes one – and that one would be statistically weird if it *didn't* happen – to make you forget about the millions of other non-events. This is called confirmation bias. We can easily close our eyes or ignore any pertinent facts that we deem momentarily necessary. "It's true. I can *feel* it." *Can* you feel it? I'm sure you feel something. As we now know, it is not true that you "felt it" – rather, it was a statistical inevitability.

Petitionary prayer – besides being base, wicked, and the Heisman of all ridiculous concepts – is another example of ignoring the evidence for a "gut feeling." How many times does a failed prayer need to occur before we start separating fact from fiction, *believing* from *knowing*? Years of unanswered prayers will go completely ignored when Sally's cancer goes into remission. The Doctor's part is, of course, ignored and goes unthanked. The new drugs, the environmental change, the simple passage of time and bodily progression (and all variables unknown) are summarily ignored. Thank you, dear deity. I will ignore the years of grief and unanswered prayers. I will ignore the emergence - and continued existence - of cancer in the first place (in Sally, or in anyone else). I will ignore that starving babies die by the thousands each week. I will ignore the natural disasters and their sickening death toll. I will ignore the facts and blindly accept belief in its place. I will ignore this paragraph concerning cognitive bias and dissonance.

Another poignant and palpable example of the confusion of language is self-importance or self-appointment. People really feel as if they deserve certain things. By this I do not mean deserving a job or a position or a contested victory (or whatever) that is assessable by rational or empirical means. In those cases, an evidential method of contesting those outcomes would be available. One could point to their work or attitude, or could point to their opponent's lack of said attributes. That is fair. No, what I am talking about is a *cosmic deserve*. "I *deserve* to be treated with dignity. I *deserve* to have a better life." This is another idea that falls flat and makes little sense. In the first case, one may feel like a courteous reciprocity is in order. You do good things, so you should be treated with more dignity. Who, exactly, is returning the favor? Who is reciprocating? An individual? Everyone? Is the universe doing the honors? Maybe you give clothing to charities, and last week you held the door for a good five or six people. Why, and wouldn't you believe, not a one of them said thank you? I *deserve* more respect. Where is my return on investment?

Maybe certain individuals in certain situations *should* have favors returned. But nobody *deserves* anything of this sort. A better life, you ask? Who doesn't want a better life? There are obviously many who *need* one. However, *deserving* one makes no rational sense. This is a useless word when angling for generalities such as better lives or the preservation of our dignity. None of us are special. It makes no sense to think of oneself as special or deserving when millions are, and will remain, destitute and dejected (financially, emotionally, mentally, physically, and socially).

Not expecting a return on investment will leave many people much happier. This is because they are not constantly sitting around waiting on some good news. Open the door, provide for charity, and be good to the environment, but do not expect a reward – in this life or some ill-conceived second one. You may be the best person in the world, and get nothing for your efforts (save, perhaps, an early death by rare and obscene accident – think, falling in a bathtub). Conversely, you may be wicked and uncaring and a cheat, and you may lead a long, mirthful, and magnificent life. Such is the way things are. (One just need open their eyeballs and watch any news channel to confirm any of this). Sometimes there is no temporal fairness, and the idea of cosmic - karma-induced - fairness hardly makes sense. *"Deserving"* falls apart in light of simple observation.

I have hopefully made obvious the importance of noticing our language and definitions, at least via a few short examples. Although certain instances and particularities sometimes do not matter much, the distinction as a whole matters immensely. Getting slogged down in our cultural lexicon can leave unpleasant scars and unnecessarily piercing questions. Separating belief from facts is important. If a woman states that she is not certain about a particular proposition, but *believes* it to be so - based on whatever - she is then in the clear. That is an honest answer. She just needs to be careful not to claim facts or the truth in its place. (And facts are indeed the only "truth" worth discussing – for those into Rorty-esque antiessentialism[4], or for those neo C.S. Lewisites who gleefully spread truthiness.)

At some point it became anathema to admit ignorance. Or, perhaps, it was always the case. Either way, it's a bad policy. If we do not know something then we should admit as much. If we as a population, culture, and *world* are to continue our shared success and survive indefinitely, we have to stop pretending we know things we do not. We have to stop pretending we know we get another do-over after this life has ceased. We have to stop pretending we know we get seventy-two horny virgins after being

---

[4] Obviously, as an existentialist, I hold firm with Rorty in rejecting Platonic essentialism (in the form Plato would have used), but I part sharply with Rorty in his hard relativist conception of epistemic points and his line on "justificatory beliefs."

martyred. We have to keep our finger off the button realizing there is probably no second chance, and that we will not be enjoying a subsequent lunch with Jesus. We may believe these things, but conflating knowing and believing causes irreparable damage and long-lasting grief. Remaining open to possibilities and change can help us relax and enjoy life a little more fully. We have to accept what we know, what we *can* know, and what we *don't now* know (perhaps *ever* know), and what the best methods of answering problems and solving dilemmas are. We also have to understand our limits on self-importance. Be confident, but do not put yourself in a position to ask questions about cosmically deserving something, or perhaps your due cosmic relief fund. The less we worry about such things, the more engaged we become in this life. It is so much easier to be happy in this way. As a collective unit – a species fighting for future survival – we need to understand and be comfortable with our limits as well as our potential. Through honest assessment and pursuance of real *truth* – the only game in town – we cannot only create a better world, but we can also understand ourselves. We can be truly happy with who we are and what we can become. We can become more engaged in our lives simply by paying closer attention to our language; that is, what we say, what it actually means, and how it affects our thoughts.

I have included a sidebar example of how deconstructing our language might work. I feel this will help bring light on how to approach this matter in the future. Now I turn to chapter five where I take a look at the language of others. How do we function in this age of information? How do we know what to take seriously? These questions are a perfect starting place for becoming more engaged in life and leading a happier existence. We are already doing a better job and are hopefully feeling more prepared to take on life. Shall we move forward, then?

Philosophical treatise on the supernatural: a linguistic analysis

...intellectually we stand on an islet in the midst of an illimitable ocean of inexplicability. Our business in every generation is to reclaim a little more land.

– T.H. Huxley

Above is a great quote concerning our view of science, our telescope into the unknown, and our goggles with which to find answers - to find the truth. There are many ideas that subvert our attention from this pursuit using glitter and antiquated hat tricks. It is very easy to become an unwilling puppet sustained by invisible strings. It is also easy to subsume ideas of supernaturalism within the category of mystery, or even science - both cases being erroneous. I write and care a lot about science and demonstrable methods of achieving results. I want now, though, to discuss the linguistic and logical failure of any notion of the supernatural. One need not tread that far into the scientific, empirical waters. We can throw out the idea of the supernatural by simply analyzing our statements.

Some things we know, and some things we don't know. This is painfully obvious. I've been a vehement champion for the reintroduction and reinvigoration of science in regards to our public conception (and reception.) We know how to approach mysteries. Mysteries lack an explanation. In no way does a lack of explanation merit an invocation of the supernatural. The supernatural, in the former case, is actually being invoked as an explanation. So, now, we have a linguistic and definitional absurdity; that is to say, no explanation = an explanation, which is nonsensical (following basic sense and, if you need it, the Aristotelian logical principle of contradiction).

So, the supernatural is an explanation. But is it really a good one? Let's evaluate that for a minute. What is it exactly that is being elucidated by invoking some cause that is *super* natural, that is to say, outside of what we know to be natural? The precedent set by A.J. Ayer and the school of logical positivism was one of linguistic analysis. What do our words mean? Are we making sense? According to this school of thought, if our statements are not falsifiable - that is, if they cannot possibly be proven false by any commensurate means - then those statements are neither true nor false, but instead literally *meaningless*. (They would break information into analytic and empirical categories. Analytic information would be trivial, because the knowledge is contained right there in the definition. Empirical knowledge is informative, as we learn about something in or about the world. That can then be either true or false. If there were no way in which to prove it false, it would then be rendered meaningless.) In certain situations there can be no real discussion of something being true or false, because certain statements are absolutely meaningless[5]. I provide some examples below.

If I make the claim, "the sky is green," we can falsify that claim if necessary. Likewise, through empirical science, we can investigate the verity or falsity of (say) chemical reactions. On the other hand, if I make the claim, "Krishna is an avatar of Vishnu," we are left with nothing observable, testable, or otherwise commensurate or connected to reality. All we have are terms based on alignments with imagination (or story, or hearsay). Is it false, or maybe true? We cannot even tread that far into the claim because, as stated, we have a meaningless setup. Nothing in the previous claim has definable terms insofar as the real, testable

---

[5]   Sir Karl Popper, established philosopher of science in the twentieth century, proposed the same principle of falsifiability to scientific discovery.

world is concerned. On the other hand, everyone can attest to the universality of chemical reactions (as well as to their definitional foundation.) If I say, "my blue unicorn has a skewed, hexagonal body shape like that of a Picasso piece," you would realize it was a meaningless statement. But, more importantly, you would realize that because it is a meaningless *invention*. I used familiar words and descriptive terms, combined them, and formed an amalgam - but this amalgam is nonsense. This is also what happens with words like "ghosts" and "demons" and "spirits."

When speaking of a "ghost," for instance, one may try to provide a description. One may describe this ghost using familiar colors or possibly our notion of transparency. Perhaps the ghost is "smoky," and maybe emits a "cold temperature" and an altogether "creepy vibe." Does anyone see what is going on here? Every description of this supposedly supernatural entity is, in fact, *natural*. I submit we would have *no idea* of what or how to conceptualize the supernatural. Even the phrase itself is nonsense. All that we ever do, say, think, or conceptualize - regardless of how fantastical it is - is done within a *natural* paradigm. Blue, cold, and smoky are all natural, human-defined characteristics. If there indeed were some entity that was supernatural, we would have absolutely no means of discussing or describing "it." No human conception - which is to say, no conception we know of - could provide an understanding (and especially discourse) for something other than the *natural* world, for that is all we know.

So, we find that the "ghost" cannot be defined with anything other than natural descriptors. We have natural definitions and terms - because that is all we possess - to describe everything.

We are now left with two choices: the ghost is then natural, or it is non-existent. If the ghost were natural we would be able to test its existence. Some test(s) would explain what we see or feel. It turns out that science has provided tests and explanations for such "apparitions" or "visions," as well as what we "feel." These experiences, as it turns out, are natural and very real. But then there is nothing *supernatural* about it. No one denies human experiences, but these experiences are not ghosts, spirits, or anything otherworldly. We would not, as I have shown, be able to even conceptualize such otherworldly, supernatural ideas in the first place. I will show it again. Right now I want you to think of describing the Christian view of God. Think hard. Give me one description that is not broken into natural descriptive terms – think of terms such as "good," "loving," "large," "powerful," etc. Recall my blue, hexagonal unicorn. We are using the color blue, geometrical shape, a horse, and a horn to describe something that is nonsensical (and non-existent) - but you knew all the descriptive units, didn't you?

To talk about ghosts, spirits or, in general, the idea of the supernatural, is not to speak of claims on truth or falsity, but is literally *meaningless*. (Although I still like having a scientific and historical discussion of such matters.) Our lives, experiences, and definitions do not let us escape or jettison the natural world in lieu of something else. Ghosts are not natural either, because we would be able to test their spatio-temporal components, their characteristics, and we would see them in stadiums - not just on heavily edited television shows with high ratings. (Ask yourselves if you actually see or learn anything "ghostly" on those shows – which, is to say, not natural. Noises? Oh, no! Noises don't exist in the real world!) So, if ghosts are not natural, then they do not exist. Neither do demons, angels, spirits, Loch Ness, Sasquatch, dragons, fairies, etc. In discursive terms, "supernatural" is a word and idea that is devoid of meaning to us.

Thinking about the language is all that was needed to nip that in the bud. Think about it. And then analyze those thoughts.

CH. 5 AGE OF INFORMATION

> If irrational beliefs weren't so often dangerous and
> a drag on human progress, you would never hear
> a peep from me about anyone's beliefs. The way I
> see it, promoting reason and skepticism is a moral
> issue. It's about caring for your fellow humans.
> — Guy P Harrison

If you notice people on electronic devices then congratulations, because you are among the select few who are able to take a step back from the madness and look in on it from the outside. It is impressive to witness, no? Today it is difficult to even perceive an "outside" to this way of life. It is not at all weird to be thoroughly sucked into the whirlwind of electronic living, enjoying digital gadgetry of all sorts. Walking down the street one can find oneself in a veritable sea of ambulatory zombies (or, even in the face of the endangering sea of statistics, vehicular zombies) consumed in their devices as they move to work or wherever. The day is simply incomplete without our unseemly daily intake of news from the world: news from our friends on social media outlets, as well as that other news. (I hesitate to use examples of social media in the view that things may be different for my future readership. "Siliconbook": for the day that digital chips replace our faces.) Our extreme myopia with this technology is not unfathomable; well, it's not anymore. And, interestingly enough, our myopia is leading us excitingly to a non-myopic place. That is a weird statement; so let me explain what I mean.

"Myopic" would appear to be the word I am looking for. Maybe "solipsistic" would fit, also. These descriptors could be apropos, but they do not necessarily have to be this way. Although an unhealthy consumption of the World Wide Web and digital gadgetry can lead us to ignore the outside world at our peril, it can also lead us to become *more* engaged. This depends on the individual. The world really is at our fingertips.

So, the problem then becomes "do we have too much information, or do we have entirely too much information?" We often feel we have so much – and can obtain it so quickly - that we shut down and ignore all of it. The attitude may betray an interesting psychological trend. "I can get almost *any* information at almost *any* time, so I will be sure to check that out later." There is no urgency in a world with urgently pressing technology. Look how fast we can go! Scheduling is rampant, but dogged planning is unnecessary. The future happens now, so there is no need to plan for it. Since this appears to be the case, we feel that we can pick and choose when and what to know and how much we should care about it. Pounded into our skulls is every possible spin and scenario on every possible speck of news. It is almost too much to bear. The result is many people tune out, and many others pretend they are experts at what they know nothing about. They are, to borrow a used phrase, "armchair experts." (In this case, though, "armchairs" may be a bit too upscale. Perhaps "used loveseat" would be a better analogous representative.)

One source has the Internet use in North America - as up to the summer of 2012 – at 273.8 million (out of an estimated 348,280,000 total people). Europe had 518.5 million (out of approximately 820,918,440) and Asia clocked in at a whopping

1076.7 million users (out of approximately 3,922,066,990). 166,029,240 Americans (in the United States) use – or at least have an account – on Facebook. Another source has the units of smartphones in worldwide circulation at just over a billion (calculated to be around 3.3 billion by 2018). I just want to point out a few more statistics before we move on. A Pew research study found the following (as of April 2012):

> "67% of cell owners find themselves checking their phone for messages, alerts, or calls — even when they don't notice their phone ringing or vibrating. 44% of cell owners have slept with their phone next to their bed because they wanted to make sure they didn't miss any calls, text messages, or other updates during the night. 29% of cell owners describe their cell phone as "something they can't imagine living without."

Unsurprisingly (unless you presumed a higher figure), 55% of cell users in 2012 used the Internet on their phones – almost doubling the figure from just three years prior.

Cable News networks – the 24-hour variety – have massive viewerships. I won't throw any more statistics at you (me in high school math class, and even now: "ah, are those numbers? Snore") but you, Dear Reader, can easily find stats on the popularity of these networks. More frightening, though, is that people actually take seriously what they hear on these networks. If you want to enjoy a fun night in, get on the Fox News and MSNBC websites. Go to the respective comment sections – any comment section will do. You will find that at each website the same disparaging things are being said about the other. Words like "brainwashed" and "spin" and "bogus" and "lies" are at the forefront of such discourse. Remember how in the last chapter we learned to focus on our language. You will start to notice when others play with words and use them inappropriately as well.

The question may arise, "how do I know what to trust and take seriously?" or "from whom do I gather accurate information?" (If these questions arose, you are already a few steps ahead of the loyal fan base of the aforementioned networks. High five.) There is a certain way to think about these things. We have to become functional skeptics, but we also have to steer clear of conspiracy theories. There is a very important difference between the two. Being a skeptic takes work, of course. We do have to put in a seemingly ceaseless amount of legwork. It is worth it.

The difference between skeptics and conspiracy theorists is not simply one of degree; degree, that is, of general incredulity – although there is certainly a noticeable difference in that area. The most salient difference is in that of response to information. The reactionary nature of conspiracy theorists is both alarming and sickly amusing. Responding to information is a process that no one can reasonably hope to escape, but the way – and degree – in which one does this, is clearly indicative of the mind one possesses. Conspiracy theorists simply do not know when to turn it off – indeed they do not even understand what "it" is. The only similarity between skeptics and the batty conspiracy theorists (shortened for the remainder as CT) is the purposive search for substantive meaning, or *real* meaning. This fact would set these groups apart from another group, the idle brains, for which any information would be "good enough." The individuals who childishly imbibe whatever information happens upon them from any quasi-authoritative source lack not the ability to fine-tune their incredulity, but instead lack whatever sparks it took for the rest of us to begin furrowing our brows. Perhaps "lack" is not the right word. But for whatever reason, no forthcoming event has yet instantiated these folks' curiosity – curiosity about what is happening, and has happened, in the world around them. This curiosity can reach such rewarding philosophical and practical depths. One thing, though, that both the CTs and idle brains have yet to fully embrace (and, it would seem, the former have completely eschewed) is the role science and evidence play in harnessing truth. Let us look at these three groups in turn.

First: the skeptics. It is good to be a skeptic. Skepticism is what gets us through life safely (although many would choose to simply ignore this important fact). Skepticism led to the rise of science, and also led to the watchful eye that fell upon religious bullying (and factual errors and contradictions and general nonsense). Skepticism - both directly and indirectly - led to the ultimate fall of monarchical Europe[6], and continues to fight and end the suppression of personal and political liberty worldwide. Skepticism is the reason for such disparate, yet beautiful and necessary discoveries, such as the germ theory of disease (as opposed to the prevalent and ought-sought-after nuisance of witchery) and refrigeration (Coors Light is forever indebted – the temperature of their beverage apparently being its only redeeming quality). Living life "as a skeptic" is really a meaningless phrase. Being a skeptic is not an attribute of note, nor does it define a person. Being a person who *thinks skeptically* is an idea that makes more sense. Note the subtle difference there. Each person can lead whatever life he (sticking with "he" as my pronoun, for the sake of simplicity) chooses, while also remaining skeptical about things. "Where," one might boldly inquire, "does it then end?" "Can we reasonably hope to avoid the total chaos of questioning everything?" My answer to this is the questioning never ends. Sometimes the sheer number of questions and ideas can be alarming. Unlike the CT,

---

[6] I leave out constitutional monarchy.

though, skeptics do not concoct nonsensical "facts" that, as it turns out, happen not to be there. Here, the CT and the idle brain share a striking similarity: they both end up believing bullshit; the CT fabricating it in bold form, and the idle brain simply accepting it (typically, in Shakespearian form, *from* the CT).

The trail left in the wake of the conspiracy theorists is both evident and, I'm a bit at pains to say, admirably consistent. The obnoxious allure is, as I said, amusing which, in turn, makes it guiltily endearing. There is, I guess, something to say for trying. The CT, however, can be dangerous – if, for no other reason, that the idle brain will accept with alacrity the garbage being spewed wholesale. We, as part of a globalized and fully integrated social structure, are not at a loss for bad information. Indeed, we always seem to have a dismaying abundance of it.

There is good news. Take heart. They are easy to spot, the bat-eared loons. The CT will babble on for minutes on end about an incoherent variety of things that he believes to be "connected." Alas, one of the hallmarks of the corrupted mind – connecting dots where no connection exists (and, in many cases, no dots). The most salient feature is perhaps the extreme paranoia in which he is irretrievably entrenched. Some one or thing is always "out to get you." I mean, haven't you noticed? For many people, aliens (who, at one point, ostensibly visited the famed Area 51) appear to have the impressive means to celestially wiretap our human minds, and the means and interest to probe other biological hotspots (paging Freud…). Another area of contention is the realm of politics. The government – or, rather, Big Brother – is out to destroy everything, didn't you know? The political left wing has had their share of quacks; namely, the 9/11 "truthers." But more profuse have been the recent litany of right wing dolts, claiming that the government (and the ill-intentioned President), if not directly bent on destroying American livelihood, is slightly inclined to tyranny. Thrown around also are terms that, unfortunately for the historically aware, have been so misused they might well have acquired new official definitions. Everyone is simultaneously a communist and a Nazi (antithetical ideologies…but hey, who's really paying attention?[7]). Vaccine nightmares to "Frankenfoods" to "inside jobs" (to: use your imagination) have been the topics of CTs' scorn. ("It smells 'fishy' in here." What? This is a vegetable garden! Open a window or something, and get a life in the process.) Oft written is the excoriating, and largely inchoate, op-ed style piece that indignantly refuses to consider the entirety of the scientific evidence (or the method) concerning a topic as necessary counterweight to some pieces of tenuous information. This is due in large part by people's discomfort of ignorance. It

---

[7] If I may, I will indulge myself for a moment. To be perfectly fair, both the two greatest twentieth century totalitarianisms – fascism and communism (more specifically, Nazism and Stalinism) – shared one interesting undertone; nationalism. Now, no more needs to be said in the case of fascism. But this is sometimes a surprising element when considering communist ideology. Nationalism was anathema to Marx, and both Maoism (China) and Marxism-Leninism (Russia) were aberrations of Marxist theory. Neither Russia nor China were sufficiently industrialized by the turn of quarter century – a prerequisite, according to Marx, for the revolution: the natural overthrow of the bourgeois class by the proletariat, or working class. In Marx's quasi-Hegelian view, the economic determinism that pushed the world along would inevitably lead to this clash of class. But Mao Zedong in China, and his Russian equivalent before him, V.I. Lenin, used nationalism as a rallying cry for revolution. They felt no longer the need to wait. This was especially true in China. The Chinese countryside was swept away in nationalist fervor, in favor of communist revolution, so that it may throw off the Western imperial yoke (there was of course Sun Yat Sen's GMD nationalist party as well). In this sense then, both communists and fascists, although exchanging vituperations as well as gunfire, shared a common thread in an undergirding nationalism. I'll go ahead and say I doubt that the likes of Glenn Beck would appreciate the hermeneutics or exegesis of the subject.

doesn't feel right *not* to have an opinion, or to defer to another more knowledgeable source. Another reason for the bountiful nature of CT opinions – and the ease of their diffusion – is simply the global stage on which to display them. The Internet allows for the effusion (and promulgation and proliferation) of *any* idea. Anyone with a keyboard can project any inane and ignominious idea that one, in a frenzy of deluded paranoia or whatever else, chooses. I invite the CT to rejoin reality. Scientific fact and method is where we draw the line. Ignoring the closest thing we have to the truth (found by way of the scientific method) is not a road to true skepticism; it is reckless off-roading on the nearest, muddiest path. Sometimes the answers are just not to be found. We have to be fine with that, and we have to learn to live with that without pretending to know things we do not. Real skeptics are skeptical of conspiracy theories. Christopher Hitchens once said, "a theory that explains everything explains nothing." The original conception of Post-Modernism (before it was hijacked by the liberalized whirlwind of cultural and philosophical relativism) was incredulity toward meta-narratives. In other words, stop connecting dots that are not there!

(Interestingly enough for Americans, the paralyzing fear of government authority is no match for that well-known heavenly despot. And typically, the ones in this vein, promoting political and personal individualism, are the very ones who, in ingratiating fashion, propitiate the God of Abraham, and wish nothing more than to ultimately live in a celestial North Korea, praising the Dear Leader from dawn till dusk. What can I say? Life would be dull without irony.)

Finally, we come to the idle brains. This group is simple. The idle brains really do nothing more than partially integrate what someone else has given them. Whatever information may come their way is simply either accepted or tossed aside. Thinking is often an inconvenience, if not a painful experience. Learning to accept certain premises and move on is admittedly a difficult process. It is a process, though, that is essential to obtaining a true happiness and navigating the path to truth - even if an off-roading detour occasionally presents itself.

To think skeptically and question everything is not to devolve into a hysterical conspiracy theorist (who's penchant for apocalyptic or eschatological reasoning is a running contender for most pervasive annoyance of the century). Something else to note is that skeptics are ok with not having the answer. Searching for the right answer – via fair, objective reasoning and the scientific method – is the process by which the most happiness and truth is obtained. The process of discerning the veracity of specific claims (differentiating between skeptics and CTs, say) is itself the result of a healthy skepticism. There isn't any way around the obvious assertion, here. A consistent skepticism is the only way any community of individuals can achieve solidarity – solidarity in thought, politics, medicine, cosmology, or anything else. We cannot weigh evidence enough, even if it takes a lifetime to do so. To do anything else is intellectually dishonest. Ignorance is ok. Willful ignorance is not. The fabrication of outlandish truth claims is not only an insidious palliative to intellectual integrity, but it is also poses a dangerous threat to society because of its availability. We all have a civic duty to shed our idle brains, toss aside any inclination toward conspiracy, and become functional skeptics.

Accepting the role technology has to play in our information is not just important; it is imperative. It seems that most people between about sixteen and fifty have no problem accepting this fact (although I suggest you look at the research to confirm such stats). Part of being in control – which is what I talked about in chapter two – is accepting and harnessing the role technology plays in our gathering and understanding information. While it is probably not healthy to be a nut about always having our phones nearby, or that we simply watch nuts on 24-hour "news" networks, it is pretty sensational that any of us can get almost any information that we so desire. We have to be skeptical and we have to put in plenty of legwork and digging, but the alternative – not having enough access to global information – is an unappealing one. Now, it may be true that so much easily accessible information may cause a sort of mental shutdown or entombment – a paralysis from analysis deal. And it may be true that this type and this speed of accessing technology are changing our brain structure and response to information (there are probably plenty of books and thousands of studies on these issues). We have to learn to roll with those punches. In a world where we are in control of ourselves and our language and our response to information, it should be worth the effort to understand the world around us more fully. We now live in a globalized, integrated society; a trend that does not show any signs of reversing. This is another perfect example of becoming engaged in life. Parsing informational specifics – and being able to do so with a healthy skepticism - will help lead to a stronger feeling of control and emotional soundness.

If we think about information in great depth, what does that tell us about the time we spend doing it? How do we allot our time? Are we busy, or do we have free time? How does time affect our lives, and why does it even matter? These are all very important questions, and they are questions that are often swept aside or ignored (ironically, because we do not have the time to worry about them). Good questions, though - like bad film quotes – recur often and should at least be considered. For instance, do you now have time to read chapter six?

Ch. 6 ABOUT TIME

> But at my back I always hear
> Time's winged chariot hurrying near;
> And yonder all before us lie
> Deserts of vast eternity
> – Andrew Marvell from *Coy Mistress*

It's hard enough to make it through the day on time. Let us say nothing of considering that time in abstract terms. But that is what I intend on doing (call me a sadomasochist, then). I think it is an immensely important thing over which to brood. Once you start considering it, it becomes such a mind-bending and exciting topic – so much so that it is much more rewarding than that old provincial banality that is the daily schedule. The concept of time – and the full consideration of its effects – is something that ineluctably affects us all at our very core. Time is luminescent. Time is amorphous. Time is everlasting and indestructible. Time is beautiful. Time may be a figment of our imaginations?

There is no such thing as time (so you should ignore the clocks and read away). I should qualify that statement. There is no tangible, concrete thing that is time. But time still exists in a very real sense and time, in this sense, is immutable. The idea of time certainly affects us in every measure and at every possible turn. So, in that way, it is certainly real. Some argue for religion's utility in the same way. The difference is we could get on without religion, but we cannot move on without time. Indeed, even the phrase "move on," is itself a reference to the passage of time.

We set our lives by clocks. External clocks are everywhere around us, consulted at almost every point of the day. Internal clocks, in another sense, do the dirty work for us. Our biological systems have evolved (with respect to light sensitivity) to manage an internal clock that, in most circumstances (certain gene mutations aside), continues to run even when we don't have access to external clocks. We are up at day, and we are down at night. What would it mean to jettison the concept of time? Let us answer another question first. What would it mean to jettison our basic sense of *daily* time?

There have been experiments conducted where certain individuals have spent considerable time in places such as caves with no instrument to dictate the passage of time. In one famous instance, one experimenter had only food, some basic shelter, artificial light, and a phone. The phone was only used to call his colleagues to apprise them of time slept and a daily log of activities. The time, of course, was only estimated. At one point he called them before and after he slept, noting he had taken one of his usual ten-minute catnaps. His colleagues had later informed him that he had been sleeping not ten minute intervals but in eight hour chunks. His calendar estimation, needless to say, was far from accurate.

We cannot seem to survive without the clock. And we are now hardwired by an internal clock as well. To think is to think in terms of the passage of time. As a lover and student of history, I deal in the business of time; the timeline is a home away from home. Time is everything to us, and yet there is no actual time. We can say time began when the universe started – it's a bit weird, but it is about all we have. It doesn't make sense to speak of time before time. Think about it for a minute. (It is profoundly annoying when theologians utter the characteristically unscientific phrase, "the 'time' before the universe began." How does that work, exactly?) However, we run into another problem. There were obviously no clocks until there *were* clocks. It took humans, bearing witness to it, to harness the idea of time – the passage of moments. We run into the situation of the tree falling in the forest – if there is no one there...

We also run into the issue of relativity. I'll give two examples. Light from a distant star is only reaching us after light years of travel. The light we are witnessing from distant stars is showing us a picture of that star long ago (it varying, of course, depending on how distant the star). If sentient creatures are seeing light from our planet from so many light years away, they might be witnessing the peak of the dinosaurs. There are obviously no dinosaurs now. We see that time is relative. It is also relative in biological terms. About 1.8 million years ago we start to see the emergence of our ancestor, homo erectus. About 200,000 years ago is the time we start to see the emergence of modern homo sapiens. If we travelled back in time 200 million years, we would see our fishy ancestor. But at no point during the actual lives of these creatures was there one creature that was born of a new species. Only through the passage of immense time can we notice the changes from natural selection pressure. It is similar to growing from a child to teenager, teenager to middle aged, and middle aged to old. That process clearly happens, but at no point do we wake up middle aged or old. Only through the process of time can we witness this change. So, again, time is relative. Time is truly awesome.

I think, though, with all that time does to affect us, we essentially ignore it. This is a mistake. It comes as no real surprise. We subconsciously realize we are doing this, and yet we have cleverly tricked ourselves into subverting our cognizance of time and pretending we have a bounty of it. It is evidently too painful to come to terms with our mortality and that our time must eventually end. Worse than that, our time ends but time itself never ends (until there are no beings left to perceive it). Christopher Hitchens once cleverly put it like this (paraphrased): You are tapped on the shoulder and told you must leave the party. But it's slightly worse – you have to leave, but the party will be going on without you. I believe Hitchens is correct in that assessment. (The quest for immortality is the topic of chapter seven.) This enterprise of self-deception leads us to an unfortunate outcome: we waste that most precious commodity in the very effort to forget about it.

We try to forget about time passing by filling every possible second of it. We have created a culture where every second of our precious time must be used, reused, and over-stimulated. Our meaningful discourse has become either so balkanized as to render it useless, or it is simply discarded on the front end. Our few decades in the sun are quickly becoming denuded of any real content. It is easier to punch the clock, fill up the time, and get out of town than it is to contemplate the day we must invariably "get out of town." The real beauty lies in the moments in between. It lies in the moments we simply count down that time, enjoying, tasting, feeling, and appreciating every single moment. We might consider turning off the television, putting down the phone, cutting off the power to our computers and electronics, and our conversation should cease to be so tastelessly stultifying. We should either spend our time exploring bigger, more important, and potentially painful issues, or we should just enjoy a contemplative state of nothingness. We could sit silently and allow ourselves to transcend the concept of "self." At this point we simply become aware of our surroundings. We become aware of the mere passage of time. We don't run from it. We don't waste it. We embrace it, use it, and appreciate it. I think it is about time that all of us embrace, use, and appreciate time – this amorphous, beautiful, and everlasting but – in our case - fleeting thing known as time. It is physically unreal or intangible, but it is about time we realize that does not matter, and that there is no excuse for not using it wisely.

This has a lot to do with how we use our time concerning the intake of information. I believe it is healthy to simply stop and notice the mere passage of time (meditation, for instance, is a good example of this), but if we are engaged in activity it might as well be worthwhile. All of what we have discussed so far can be tied together in living a more engaged life. How happy we could be when we learn to accept certain events while remaining patient and in control. How happy we would be learning that some things "just happen" and that we are not special. How happy we would be if we understand what we, and others, mean by our words and also how to approach those words in the context of the plethora of global information. The discussion and conception of time leads to yet another weighty topic that affects us all: our quest for immortality. This issue is one that causes much unnecessary distress and discomposure. With this in view, we now turn to chapter seven.

CH. 7 THE QUEST FOR IMMORTALITY

"My name is Ozymandias, king of kings:
Look on my works, ye Mighty, and despair!"
Nothing beside remains. Round the decay
Of that colossal wreck, boundless and bare
The lone and level sands stretch far away"
– Percy Bysshe Shelley

Vain is the ambition of kings
Who seek by trophies and dead things
To leave a living name behind
And weave but nets to catch the wind
– John Webster from *All the Flowers of the Spring*

What is clear to everyone is that we all die. Most of us also push this fact into the deep recesses of our minds. We spend most of our time doing two things. We reject our immanent death (in various degrees and methods of obfuscation), and we spend a great deal of time trying our hand at immortality. Throughout the course of history, time and again, we see the various attempts to have some part of ourselves live on in perpetuity. There is a great deal of commentary on these attempts as well. It might appear fatuous to ask the question, "Why do we resist our mortal cessation?" I think, in a general sense, the answer is rather obvious. But I want to dig a bit deeper here, because I think the implications are much more important than we realize.

The obfuscatory nature of the "meaning of life" is so absurd to even consider, that most people simply occupy their time in order to live peacefully. If we cannot change our collective outcome, then why worry about it? That is a fair question, and we could probably end any future discussion on the matter right here. It would be unfairly dismissive, though, to put out of mind anything that may cause consternation. Indeed, if the outcome cannot be changed, then what is the harm in simply talking about it?

Some people do deal with this matter, but they do so in a way that cleverly (or uncleverly) gerrymanders around the true implications. Religion was one clear way to placate people's fear of mortality. Why not just say that we never really die? It only appears that we die. Or you die once but don't you fret, you get another opportunity – and luckily, that one lasts forever. The notion of "eternity," which does not track reality in a scientific sense, is easily bandied about as a conceivable reality. This is interesting, because it is so starkly simple. Afraid of death? No problem. Here is eternity for you – no traceable end. The concept is nonsensical (and, in my opinion, much more frightening), but it is simultaneously endearing and understandable. Everything around us decays and ultimately ceases to live. However, I do not see this as a reason to hide behind a wall of fabricated terms or supernaturalism. I see it as an opportunity to appreciate what we have, and establish ways to make life better for everyone around us. Life is really only special *because* it ends.

I mentioned in the last chapter (talking about the concept of time) that Christopher Hitchens had likened dying to being asked to leave a party. You are tapped on the shoulder and told you must leave. But it is slightly worse than that. You are told that you have to leave, but the party is going to go on without you.

That, he believes, is what scares people most (and I agree), and that is why people concoct bogus stories and posit bogus claims about their putative immortality. Hitchens goes on to say that in the Christian relation of this immortality, you are told that you are going to another party; and this party you can never leave. The Boss also insists you have a good time. (Hitchens had a way with words that was matched by very few.) The psychologist and author, Jesse Bering, sums up the reality: "The mind is what the brain does; the brain stops working at death; therefore, the subjective feeling that the mind survives death is a psychological illusion operating in the brains of the living." Neuroscientist, philosopher and author, Sam Harris, justly mentions that we have no idea whether some form of immortality awaits us after our mortal deaths, but all of the evidence (and common sense) leads us to believe otherwise. With last regard to this form of immortality, let me quote from Stephen Cave's wonderful book, "Immortality" (a book that I strongly recommend). Cave deftly cuts the feet out from under this form of immortality: "If this life here on earth is regarded merely as a series of tests for a place in another life, then it is necessarily devalued: with eyes fixed firmly on future bliss, the immortalist fails to grasp the value of being *now*."

There is a type of quest for immortality that makes more logical and moral sense. It also makes biological sense. In fact, we seem to have little control over our predilection for this quest. I'm speaking of course about spreading our DNA. Even when considering that many adults do not want children (and that the choice do so or not is a conscious one), no one can deny the urge to spread their DNA. From an evolutionary standpoint it makes sense that we have a biological urge to do this. The goal of life – from the gene's eye view – is to propagate our DNA. The gene propagates itself. As Richard Dawkins pointed out in the 1970's with his groundbreaking book, "The Selfish Gene," individual bodies are essentially machines for shuttling genes. Once the genes are passed on, the body isn't a necessitated feature. The individual is not the unit of selection – the gene is.

But we have reached a point of cognitive awareness – as well as scientific and cultural understanding - where we can appreciate our biology, but we can make the best decisions that affect us as individuals and as a community. We no longer have to live in the shadow or under the yoke of biological Darwinism. We can voluntarily decide to do what we wish (like have children or not) without recourse to our genes' wishes. Having offspring, though, is the only real way to enjoy immortality – even though "we" will not be there to harness the experience. If you will allow me one more sojourn into the land of Hitchens, I will soon reach my conclusion. In regards to the reality of immortality, Hitchens presents one more sharp observation. "My three beautiful children are my only shot at a second life, let alone an immortal one. If I was told to do what all monotheists are told, which is to admire the man who would gut his kid to show his love for God (reference to Abraham), I would say 'No, fuck you'." I share this because the only real immortality any of us assuredly can have comes in the form of progeny.

Why do we attempt some form of immortality? Why do we attempt fame and fortune, a name and reputation that stand the test of time? Do we believe we will make the history books? The science manuals? The annals of popular culture? Do we wish our names to dance on the tongues of future civilizations? With the fact of immanent death always looming near, it comes as no surprise why we bury the idea of impending death while simultaneously formulating a grandiose plan for surviving it. It is all really a sordid business. The fact that we evolved and are just here easily displays the absurdity – or, if it sounds better, improbability - of life. But this is not something over which to pine and agonize. Quite the contrary. This is the *carte blanche* we all ultimately want. It is the most beautiful of cleared slates. We can write our own story. We cannot continue to live indefinitely. But that is precisely *why* the brevity of our own lives is so special. We can use that time wisely, or we can waste it. How profligate a notion is the idea of eternity when we can barely pass a few decades without persistent boredom? We may reach immortality via fame or a chip off the old block, but whether or not we do is a moot point. If we cannot learn to live happily with the time we have, then what does it matter if there is an additional opportunity? If you can live happily, and enjoy being a student of life, then you should simply, as Richard Dawkins puts it, give thanks "in a vacuum" for simply being around to contemplate any of this. We are profoundly lucky to simply *be*.

The quote at the beginning is an excerpt of Shelley's poem "Ozymandias." We may reach unbelievable heights in this life – social, financial, or material heights. No matter the life we lead we must realize it eventually ends. The vast, sweeping fields of our success or our control will be but barren wastelands one day. Carl Sagan exquisitely demolishes our self-importance and ultimate significance in his fantastic and timeless book, "Pale Blue Dot":

> Look again at that dot. That's here. That's home. That's us. On it everyone you love, everyone you know, everyone you ever heard of, every human being who ever was, lived out their lives. The aggregate of our joy and suffering, thousands of confident religions, ideologies, and economic doctrines, every hunter and forager, every hero and coward, every creator

and destroyer of civilization, every king and peasant, every young couple in love, every mother and father, hopeful child, inventor and explorer, every teacher of morals, every corrupt politician, every "superstar," every "supreme leader," every saint and sinner in the history of our species lived there - on a mote of dust suspended in a sunbeam."

This life needs to be cared for. In it live the ones who should be loved for all they are worth (and more). Relinquishing the quest for immortality leads to beautiful accomplishments, and it clearly leads to becoming more engaged in this crazy, absurdly wonderful life. Understanding how to live in and for the present requires we understand the endlessly important concept of history and our indissolubly connected stories. And that leads to caring for others and a more compassionate life altogether. All of this then ultimately leads to a renunciation of bad faith, bad thinking, and attachments, and it props us up for enjoying a simpler existence. These topics will serve as the remainder of the philosophy in part one.

> "An astronomically overwhelming majority of people who could be born never will be. You are one of the tiny minority whose number came up. Be thankful you have a life, and forsake your vain and presumptuous desire for a second one." - **Richard Dawkins**

> "When left to our own devices, our minds busy themselves with plans, plots, worries and idle speculation – much of it about things that might go badly for us. The capacity to think about the future is of course enormously useful, but it can also foster angst and seriously undermine our prospects of happiness. By dwelling on all manner of possible threats, we bring death into life, only then to die without having really lived." - **Stephen Cave**

CH. 8 YOU'RE HISTORY

History will be kind to me, for I intend to write it
— Churchill

Some historians hold that history is just
one damned thing after another
— Arnold Toynbee

We didn't start the fire. It was always burning
since the world's been turning.
We didn't start the fire, but when we are gone
it will still burn on and on and on
— Billy Joel

At night when you get ready to turn in and turn out the lights, you also usually turn off your computer (well, you really should because it just gets overheated). You might scroll to the top and click "clear history." All of the websites you visited that day are then erased from your computer's memories. They vanish like an Agatha Christie character. Imagine if we could do that to ourselves; or imagine if someone could do that *to* us without our knowledge. That is a frightening prospect. We are lucky that clearing our own history with a single button is not a realistic option. Many of us in moments of heated anger or impulse would click that button. We do not want to remember the drunken condition we were in the night before (our hangover ardently reminding us), much less the moments or days or years of anguish or destitution. No more demoralizing and dispiriting memories. Click. Gone.

I want come back to this idea in a moment. Let me first make a note about the title of this chapter. I decided on "you're history" because of the somewhat cutesy double meaning – as in, "you're history, chump!" and the actual fact that we are indeed history. We are our own history. Wow, sort of mind-blowing isn't it? I'll say it again. *We are our own history.* It is happening everyday. We live it day in and day out. We live our lives and make history in every moment. I also could have opted for the slightly less catchy "your history," which obviously denotes "the history of us" or that history is ours or belongs to us. (Of course, if I am taking a large Facebook or Youtube sample, I might presume that many would read the latter *as the former* and discern no difference in the very first place. One of my many woes.) My first option was "why history matters." I intend on demonstrating this point, at any rate. So, Dear Reader, you're (*you are,* for Christ sake) welcome to mull over the title for the remainder of the chapter. In fact, I suggest it.

Let us return then to the futuristic society where erasing our memories is not only an option, but also a prevalent act. Let us assume that half of the population decides to go through with this. What would it mean for those people? What would this impulsivity mean for the rest of us? What would society look like and how would it function? If individuals or communities only did it once it might not change too much for the rest of us. But let's say that once you get a feeling of "clearing the cobwebs" you cannot stop; you do it over and over every time something unfortunate occurs. If this happened, nobody would really know who they were. No concept of "us" or "we" (or even "I") would be forthcoming. We would no longer share a past or a story. We would regrettably be floating through "life" with nothing to offer anyone or ourselves. I can hardly think of anything more dystopian.

Consider this scenario. A woman approaches a younger man named Jason. She asks him about his favorite color and he cannot give her an answer. She inquires about where was born and he still cannot give an answer. She wants now to know about his future. What does he know, and what can he say? He has no clue where he has been, so his future does not make sense to ponder. The woman eventually walks away discouraged and annoyed. Jason, not being able to do much else, shrugs and moves on. He has no recourse to prior feelings or emotions – from himself or anyone else – to compare and contrast. He is an effectual zombie. He then realizes the pain from this recent encounter is (once again) too much to withstand, so he unconcernedly opens the "memory-be-gone" app on his iPhone 47, pushes the button, and is once again comfortably numb.

This scenario paints a manifestly dismal picture of our lives without history. It is purposefully dichotomized and blunt and striking. "What if," you shrewdly ask, "one could erase the bad memories only?" Okay, we can consider that. What would our lives be like with only "good" memories? Indeed, how do we even use a word like *good* without the word *bad*? The concept of either makes no sense without the other. We can *only* have good memories if we also have bad ones. Summer friendships mean nothing without the memory of falling out of that tree or cutting skin on barbwire fence jumps. Grandma's cherry cobbler on a cold Sunday morning means nothing without being deathly ill the night before from bad fish. The hug from the young sibling is obscured without concomitant fighting over the old toys. Running through the golden, sunbathed fields of wheat in late afternoon is worthless without the rainy days stuck languishing indoors. Getting that professional job full of responsibility is devoid of content without the times of dancing and barhopping with drunken strangers until the early hours of the morning (and sleeping until noon…and possibly calling Grandma for some cherry cobbler). The love that went right dissolves in the absence of the almost-loves that went wrong.

Our lives gain meaning from our pasts. Our victories and our failures, our loves and heartbreaks, our strengths and our weaknesses, our confusion and clarity, and our smiles and our tears hinge upon each other and compose our totality. We are nothing without our *everything*. You are not you without *all* of you. And we are not *us* without each other.

If this is what it means to "be our history" and to write it everyday, then history definitely matters and each of our days breathing should count for a little something. We can not only see that the attention we pay to our time spent doing or saying or thinking certain things is important, but we also see the importance of helping others understand this. If our history matters, then so does the history of the next person. We all share stories and we can learn from each other; this can make our lives more fulfilling and exciting. Most importantly, *all of us* ultimately share a story of survival – all living things share one big cosmic, evolutionary story. In this light, provincial notions of things like tribe, nation and faith are rendered puerile and insipid. Learning our history - our collective history - can lead to a better understanding of each of us; who we are, what we stand for, and why we care in the first place.

History is not deterministic. Things do not happen a certain way. They just happen. I do not mean by this that everything that has happened did so on whims or fancy. History doesn't *think*. Obviously, what people do or say affects the next point in history. This is precisely why what we do and say matters; this is what I meant when I said we *make* our history. What we *all* do determines how people will read our history, and this is why we should *choose* to act a certain way. History is important in this sense. It is not only important to study the past for its own sake (a fine pursuit, methinks), and it is not so we will not make similar future mistakes (also important). But, rather, we study and appreciate history so we can understand our human story *now.* The past does not matter for the past alone, but the past matters for the present. It matters for you and for me. Everything from the decisions we make to how we think of ourselves and our journeys (restraining from quoting Frost, here) are dictated by history.

How did Thomas Jefferson feel when writing the declaration of Independence? What did it mean to him as a human being at that time? Would it feel the same today? Put yourself in his position. If not, what would be different? Is the human experience not luminescent and everlasting? How about Napoleon's troops crossing into the Russian icy winter? What about every battle in history fought in icy or feverish hellscapes? Do we fight and suffer and die for our families, or perhaps our own lives? Do we pursue war for power, avarice, land, money, or ideology? Was FDR correct in expanding government power to help the destitute and indigent? Was Reagan right in rolling back New Deal practices and ideologies from Roosevelt through Johnson? Who were these Presidents as individuals? Think of how all of this matters when put in perspective.

What about the "what ifs" of history? What if Washington's notoriously sketchy battle record had not redeemed itself during the Revolutionary War (it very well could have been taken down another notch, and America might never have been), or what if the Cherokee were never removed and herded as chattel to Oklahoma? What if Hitler became a successful artist? What if

Trotsky instead of Stalin had taken the reins from Lenin? What if Arab "houses of wisdom" in the Middle East never passed on to the West the (essentially) lost manuscripts of ancient Greek greats such as Aristotle? What if the Renaissance never took off in Florence? What if Martin Luther decided against posting his ninety-five theses? What if the Zionists decided on Argentina instead of Palestine? I could go on and on.

This extends to our pre-history. What if a gene mutation did not lead to a funny protruding toe for the great African Apes? We would not have started to walk upright. Forget eating meat and cooking, forget bigger brains; forget the agricultural revolution, etc. The cosmos may never have awakened to know itself. I shudder at the thought. And to say history or the past is boring. That is a shameful statement, but I know it simply arises from ignorance of the true beauty of the past.

What does this say about our present? We can view historical people as people like us, and view events as events that can (and often do) occur in the present. If we are informed in the present, we can then inform our future. We do not care about history as a cautionary tale or preemptive strike for the future; we care because it matters right now. What happens *now* affects the *future*. It matters because each of us shares a past. We are *inextricably bound* to one another – both historically and biologically – whether we like or not. And we all move inexorably toward death with either more, or less, information about each other and our true selves. All we have to do is choose to know. If you care at all about life, you really are caring about history. Choosing not to know or care seems perplexing in this light.

Some say that there are no stupid questions. This, frankly, is bullshit. However, the statement is usually followed with a pernicious addition: "there are only stupid people." There may be stupid people, although this raises flags and alerts with our language detection kit. What does "stupid" mean, exactly? Typically, one finds this is a stand-in for "ignorance." There is nothing wrong with ignorance, just (as I said before) with willful ignorance. I once heard as a student teacher one student vocalize an ostensibly "stupid" question in a high school classroom. Most teachers are annoyed with such questions. And most students do not have the *cajones* to bring up this type of generalized concern. The student cheekily and somewhat insolently asked, "Why even study history, anyway? It's just old stuff, so why does it even matter now?" The students were quiet. I smiled as I looked at my shoes. It really is a brilliant question. It is a question that absolutely matters. If we cannot ask these tough questions, then we are not truly living a meaningful life. If I had time and a platform I would have answered her question.

Historian and award winning author, David McCullough, writes in *"Why History?"* that "History shows us how to behave. History teaches, reinforces what we believe in, what we stand for, and what we ought to be willing to stand for." This is true. But I go even further and deduce the baseline premise: you're history. History is the story of us. It is the story of us, because we create it daily. And it is the story of us, because we make no sense without those who came before us and paved the way. I do not just mean they figuratively paved the way. Take a closer look at the past. You will find yourself saying "wow," quite a bit.

If we care anything about ourselves (and, to be fair, we may not – if this is you, you may stop reading now) then we have to realize that history matters. Think about how much more caring you will be toward your neighbor when you realize that we are not truly separated, historically or biologically. Championing personal responsibility is important, but this responsibility also means recognizing our responsibility toward others, responsibility toward everyone. In the film, *Cloud Atlas*, one of the futuristic characters, Sonmi-451, says this of our subject: *"Our lives are not our own. From womb to tomb, we are bound to others. Past and present. And by each crime and every kindness, we birth our future."* For a film portraying our interconnectedness through grand stretches of time, I think this concisely brilliant thought sums it up nicely.

The last three chapters in part one concern less pressing matters. Well, it isn't that they are necessarily less pressing (certainly not less important), but they discuss more simplistic measures of becoming engaged in life and being happier. We move next to the discussion of attachments. The last point I will make here is if we manage to lose ourselves in our social or financial milieus, or in material items (say), it is much more difficult to appreciate life for what it is. That includes all people in all conditions. That is our history and our past. Those are our stories. If *we* matter, then so does history. If history matters, then so does everyone around us. I'm history, you're history, we're all history. If we do not make a valiant attempt to understand this more efficiently and deeply, we may all be "history" – in the other cutesy sense of the word.

CH. 9 ATTACHMENTS

He who binds himself to a Joy
Doth the winged life destroy;
But he who kisses the Joy as is it flies
Lives in Eternity's sunrise
– William Blake *Eternity*

Gather ye rosebuds while ye may
Old Time is still a-flying
And this same flower that smiles to-day
To-morrow will be dying
– Robert Herrick from *To the Virgins, to Make Much of Time*

Much of our unassuming discomfort and unease about our lives – including, perhaps most notably, existential unease – is caused by attachment. One's life can be systematically ruined, or at least seriously tarnished, by a putatively unalterable attachment of some kind. "Attached to what?" you might proddingly ask. I've come to realize that one (and I mean to connote – or implicate – everyone) can be attached to any one thing or, in some unfortunate instances, a multitude of things. These attachments are, in many cases, unlucky byproducts of misspent time, technological proliferation, intellectual laziness, or some latent emotional dilemma being shielded and obfuscated by a "hobby." Any of us can fall victim to becoming addicted (an ostensibly "terminal" case, I dare to say, of attachment) to any number of activities or items. Below I provide a few examples of attachment, and I point out the danger of losing recognition of the self and of the present moment; becoming stone faced and unaware of the attachment's debilitating nature. Losing or eschewing attachments provides one with the requisite sanity and perspective to move through life relatively unscathed.

Of course, it is not possible, Dear Reader – as I am sure you are dutifully aware – to cross life's finish-line completely unscathed. The most trenchant of Buddhists (perhaps an odd descriptor) will be mentally, emotionally and physically scarred during the course of their lifetime. (This is especially notable in the case of the Chinese subjugation of Tibet. Many Tibetans have been forcibly removed, among much worse horror.) But letting go of attachments – both physical and emotional – has provided them an indomitable perspective to deal with such political, physical, and psychological maladies. One need not be a Buddhist or ascetic or mendicant to understand the value of being free of attachment. You can achieve this while owning things or enjoying a decent standard of living. I have also stated elsewhere that no one really needs to extol the virtues of moderation. The idea is pretty well established, and it has obvious benefits. Although moderation is not always appropriate (I argue this quite vociferously), donning a centrist perspective usually eases or eradicates unnecessary pain. Polarization and sectarianism and disputation all have their places, but there is real value in being comfortable with what you have.

I argue not that one should have *no* attachments. This would be missing my point. This would also be unrealistic. I love my family, and I am very much attached to them. But understanding when to "let go" or, say, "get out of the way" - in the case of our children - is important. That is as far as I wish to take that concept at this juncture. ("*Real*" love, and its subsequent attachment, issues more problematic concerns…for another rainy day, perhaps.)

Real progress, however, can be made on the issues of misspent time and technological proliferation. Misspent time includes time wasted *because* of technological proliferation. Now, it is not technology's "fault" (or the fault of those who create and propagate it) that many are attached or addicted to its comforts and facilities. Personal responsibility should vindicate, and clear the slate for, technology. However, it is still an issue that needs to be addressed.

Many times, addressing this issue comes in the form of a debate about how *much,* or how *strong* or *developed* our current technology is. This, in my view, is a distasteful case of barking up the wrong tree. It provides yet another scapegoat – in our culture of almost professional scapegoating – avoiding any personal responsibility or moral fortitude. Attachments to Facebook or smart phones or iPads cause so much misspent time, I am afraid to enumerate the hours available that could have been put toward productive work or leisure. (Perhaps I will inadvertently date myself with these examples if this book is read many years from now. Perhaps I am also inadvertently fooling myself to believe this will be read many years from now.) This is not an anti-technology diatribe. One can spend time with technology without becoming attached.

So, Dear Reader, you may then ask if *productive* work or leisure can also assume the insidious roll of "attachment." Indeed it may. I have caught myself attached – even addicted – to the seemingly benign hobby of reading and collecting books. Like anything else, my strong proclivity for learning, yearning for more books and more knowledge, developed into an attachment. I still struggle with this attachment. Others may struggle with similarly noble attachments – musical perfectionists, dancers, chefs, gardeners, sculptors, artists, or whatever else. Frivolity need not be a prerequisite for developing unhealthy attachments. The benchmark here is clinging too strongly to these things without being able to let go.

Attachments of any kind cause pain. Once one does not have access to that of which (or what or whom) they are attached, the longing can be tremendously painful, even physically unsettling. It may prove difficult to simply let go of the attachment (well, that's a bit of a truism and platitude, is it not?), but that is about as simple as one can make it. There is no twelve-step process by which we "learn" to "let go." In fact, that sort-of processed effort defeats the purpose. Excluding physical addictions (such as alcoholism), *attachments* must simply be left to founder and toil on their own. And much like a parasite, an attachment will not survive without host. Making the decision "not to care" about not having our way with a certain attachment, at any particular moment in time, is difficult but certainly possible. Not caring is even a bit of a mischaracterization. One may still *care*, but still realizes letting go is the only viable and lasting alternative. Indeed, just letting go – resigning to drop the attachment - is the only way to become immediately happy. Learning to do this throughout one's life makes one consistently happy.

Try enjoying the present moment without judgment. Enjoy it no matter what it brings. Stay with the moment, and tell yourself "this is it." If "this is it," then being "ok" or "not ok" is really beside the point. This is not a clarion call to nihilism or defeatism or even determinism. We will not always dwell in some euphoric, utopian state of happiness, and "letting go" will not always work or be sufficient. In some cases, not resigning, not passively or actively "settling," but fighting and passionately striving, is the right path to pursue. As I have said before, however, being in control consists in large part of realizing and accepting the almost constant *lack* of control.

If we can learn to "let go" of our attachments, realize and accept the transience and ephemeral nature of life's circumstances (as well as its apathy to our comfort level), we can then start the process of getting on with our lives. We can be wakeful, attentive, and "alive" to each moment and each experience. This idea applies to everyone. One need not subscribe to Buddhist principles (especially the extraneous superstitious ones) to come to value the meditative and contemplative virtues. Attachments can germinate and be fostered in any environment, even seemingly benign ones. Be careful to notice this and bear witness to the positive change it can lend your life.

Another of life's important realizations is that, along with jettisoning attachments, enjoying Mother Nature increasingly becomes a relevant happiness-inducer in our lives. The simple and permanent beauty fills a void that is left by dropping our transient attachments. Chapter ten looks at why this is the case.

CH. 10 REFLECTIONS ON NATURE

> I was born upon thy bank river
> My blood flows in thy stream
> And thou meanderest forever
> At the bottom of my dream
> — Thoreau

> Great things are done when Men & Mountains meet
> This is not Done by Jostling in the Street
> — William Blake

> In the woods, too, a man casts off his years, as the
> snake his slough, and at what period soever of life is
> always a child. In the woods is perpetual youth.
> — Ralph Waldo Emerson

The last chapter on attachments was really a short preface for this one. The two are conjoined and can be considered two parts of one bigger philosophical idea. Dropping attachments is the first step. Appreciating the simple beauty in life is the next step in the process. This can take many forms. Chapter eleven – the last in this part of the book – summarizes these ideas and probably helps answer some questions up to this point about living both simplistically and philosophically; namely, if it is indeed possible to do this. (But more on that when we get there.)

I won't sit here and tell you I am some romantic globetrotter, the quintessential woodsman, a purveyor of all things ascetic or monastic, or a stern critic of all easy comforts. However, I do believe there is a clear disparity in the things we usually do (and take for granted) and the things that can ultimately maximize and extend the longevity of our happiness. Immersing ourselves in Mother Nature provides more than just a hippie's penchant for poetry and granola; in other words, more than you might think. It can be truly life changing.

I thought I would issue that initial disclaimer, and offer an extended hand of moderately tapered normalcy. I, too, enjoy all of the technological comforts. Most people are clear about their aversion to hearing about how their laptops, phones, and PlayStations are killing their livelihood. While I believe that there is some truth to that assertion the issue is not that there is too much of one, but simply that there is not enough of the other. If it is necessary to give up some of the indoor comfort for some outdoors experience, then I think that is something that should be done. One also tends to appreciate the indoor comforts the longer one is without them. After a week in the woods or in the mountains, coming back to the iPad is a pretty sweet reward. The real reward, however, is appreciating the cathartic effects of being outdoors, and the very real possibility of temporarily ridding yourself of *your self* – and that has its own wonderful rewards.

Let me point out one important thing. Nature does not care about us. It doesn't think. It doesn't pine or cuddle or seethe or smile. Yet we ascribe to Her (along with a personalized pronoun) all of these human characteristics. This is not really noteworthy, as we humans make a habit out of anthropomorphizing everything around us. We cannot find a meaningful way to make sense of any of this planet – our surroundings or our circumstances – without recourse to *us*. (Recall Camus' idea of the Absurd.) But there is something quite disarming, untraditionally beautiful, and strangely endearing about this lack of prescience. Nature is not there for us, yet it *can* provide everything for us. In nature we find everything we need for those easy comforts to be developed in the very first place. And it still provides for us a sense of belonging – belonging to a bigger, more inclusive picture. In the great outdoors we can take in the whole panorama, a sweeping view of the solitude. This solitude provides for us a permanent place. It gives us perspective. We are simultaneously insignificant nothings, yet we all belong to a greater whole. I do not mean by this anything religious or mystical. Indeed, the real and everlasting beauty is that Nature exists apart from all of our meaning mongering, anthropomorphizing, and unnecessary added content. It is there, interminably running and recycling, aside from our good and bad moods, weddings, deaths, or reflective essays. It is precisely because our lives and reflections do nothing to affect the unalterable stoicism of Mother Nature that it is something worth speaking about. Even when our actions portend harmful results, She stands unwaveringly in the face of those results. Our resolve to save the planet, our environmental zeal, our green thumbs, and the ardor, with which we resolutely stand hand in hand with Her, do not affect the ultimate attitude of Nature – which is to say, no attitude whatsoever. She adapts and shows no concern over any state She might currently be in. So, what can this teach us?

It doesn't teach us to be unfeeling, uncaring, empty statues (although one might cull as much from Her). No, what we learn is that we are not that important; or rather, that we all share equitable levels of importance – cosmic importance (not socially or economically, but *ultimately*). The sense of *self* slowly begins to wilt and wane. Neurologically speaking, there is no "I" in there controlling the wheels, no center command, and no homunculus in a control room turning dials. Consciousness is a beautiful mystery, but a mystery that is slowly and steadily being solved. Through the practice of meditation we can learn to *be* pure experience. I say *be* because we can reach a point where there is no experiencer, no *we* in fact. The sense of self dissolves. We learn to yearn for engaging in the simple passage of moments, and for the dissolution of the self. Remember, this is no cosmic, quantum nonsense language. You do not have to be a Buddhist or Hindu – or much worse, learned in the language of Deepak Chopra – to master this practice. There is no such specialty to be procured.

Sit by a quiet river on a lazy summer afternoon. Notice the sounds of your environment. Notice the colors of the lush, verdant greenery embracing the riverbank. Be aware of physicality involved in the experience. How does the water look? How about the rocks? What about the plants and animals? Feel your breathing, and feel your body in its position. Simply pay attention to each moment. If you feel an outside thought creeping in, simply recognize it as such and go back to experiencing. You are not thinking any longer, only experiencing. You will slowly start to realize – after the fact, of course – that there is no longer any*one* or any*body* doing the experiencing. You just become *part* of the experience. When you leave this spot (it could be a mountain, the woods, a prairie, a meadow, a canyon, etc.) you will feel much more at peace with yourself. You will be a less selfish and more compassionate version of you.

Nature helps us realize our relative unimportance in the grand scheme of reality. We can recognize both the absurdity of our existence, and the beauty of Nature's perfect, inviolable insouciance. As we die and return to the Earth, we become a part of that everlasting cycle. I'm assuring you that this understanding can be enjoyed in the same light as we enjoy our Canon cameras and laptops. I am currently writing this on my Mac. And I enjoy those items much more realizing that they are but mere superfluities. As I enjoy these pleasures, I take further pleasure knowing that outside Nature continues on her path unperturbed. That is one thing I can always count on. It is one thing you can count on as well. We all share more than we realize, and that makes the planet a little smaller, a little more engaged, and little more compassionate. That is a bit of understanding that would do us all well.

Recognizing our shared past and our interconnectedness, thinking more deeply about our language and situation in life, and garnering a true humility and appreciation for the understanding that we are not as important as we thought we were: these are priceless notions about how and why to become engaged in a happy, meaningful life. "Your last chapter seems more my style. What about the simple, 'back porch' pleasures of life? Do they add anything to a happier existence?" I thought you would never ask, my Dear Reader. They absolutely do. We simply have to become engaged in those moments, and not passively let those experiences drift away unnoticed.

CH. 11 ON SPONTANEITY AND LIFE'S SIMPLE PLEASURES

All night there isn't a train goes by
Though the night is still for sleep and dreaming
But I see its cinders red on the sky
And hear its engines steaming

My heart is warm with the friends I make
And better friends I'll not be knowing
Yet there isn't a train I wouldn't take
No matter where it's going
– Edna St. Vincent Millay from *Travel*

The chapters in this book are pretty short. The book itself is pretty short. The entirety of this book is really all I had to say on the matter. Well, it's not *all* I had to say, but it is all that I felt was necessary to say at this particular time (for better or worse). I'm glad it turned out to be a readably short book. Life can be enjoyed in this way as well. Sometimes life's pleasures are simple and easy, attainable and occur often. It may be because of these reasons they are often overlooked. We need not over conceptualize life in order to be happy all of the time. We do not need philosophy all of the time, nor is the case for artistic discussions. Life's "little moments" add up and are important to have. So do not think, Dear Reader, that I am only interested in the clouds (I hope I have shown that our philosophy actually brings us back to earth and into reality).

You are correct in assuming that simple moments in life are just as important for remaining happy and sane. However, these moments do not count if they are only paid lip service in retrospect. Being engaged here is no different or less important than it is with our philosophy (our language, our understanding, and our appreciation or humility for certain things). If we can recognize how effortless and breathtaking a simple moment truly is, we can find ourselves much more perceptive to them in the future. Indeed, we can find them around every corner and almost all of the time. We do not create these moments; we only begin to recognize how prevalent they are, and then tune in to enjoy them as much as possible.

I will read lengthy tomes on history (or historiography – a more boring endeavor if you are not inclined) or other such massive catalogues of information, but I realize most people want a simple book to peruse. I do not believe this book is simple in the sense that I have provided easy to read, facile nonsense (a la our "self-help" book), but it is much simpler in its basic conception of understanding our lives. I cut through the pithy boloney, and that seems to help with its comprehensive ease. I would like to think the straightforward nature of it seems to cut a clear and lucid path to the end of the book. The point is that, in some cases, a simple, small dose of something can ultimately pack a punch or otherwise leave an indelible impression. I spend some time in this chapter pointing this out.

We should pay close attention to our language ("You're all beautiful and perfect!" – insert saccharine and unctuous smile), but what about sipping lemonade on the back porch on a summer afternoon? We should think deeply enough to recognize our place in this world and the cosmos, but what about watching the sunset cast a golden hue on a pile of soft, fallen leaves? It is invaluable to understand our connected past and to show humility and deference toward the story that played out before us, but how about simply watching the kids goggle over some toy and flash a ridiculous half-toothed smile? What about that? What about lounging on a couch, and watching some half-baked romantic comedy or infantile "horror" movie (and laughing throughout) with our lovers? What about driving on a storied backcountry road, in a sea of incandescent starlight, in the midst of crisp Fall? Add to that the smell of bonfires and faint laughter as you hear the convivial joining of friends in the fresh autumn night. What about watching the breeze blow through the flowers on a spring day? Petting the fiercely loyal dog on the bank of the mercurial river? Digging our toes into the moist sand while watching the sunrise peak over the Ocean's dreamlike horizon (insert Folgers commercial)? The possibilities are endless.

So, why do we do these types of things? We do not really "do" them, but rather they "do" us. These moments of splendid simplicity occur to us all and do so frequently. The problem is we often do not notice them while they are occurring. We may retell the story of relaxing in the rocking chair watching the sky display a resplendent pastiche of clouds, lines, and figures, but we seem not to fully embrace those descriptors. We just say something like this: "Yeah, the sky looked nice." Why? Why is that good enough? That hardly seems good enough for anybody. You did not enjoy the moment because the sky "looked cool" while you rocked in some chair. No, there was so much more happening. What *really* happened – and what you should dutifully recall – is that the smooth rhythm of the rocking in that timeworn, perspicacious wicker chair, jarred loose a sensual memory of the carefree days of your younger life. And the sky; well, the sky's warm and comforting potpourri of shapes and colors resulted in a nostalgic trip into the blurry corners of your mind, as well as your desires, fears, comforts, your confusion and clarity. It is something that changes you in the moment, and it is something that stays inside you, lying dormant in those blurry corners, until the next experience occurs. However, you simply did not care or think it important enough to engage yourself in such a way as to fully share your experiences. Even if we do not share these experiences, and even if we do not write a journal or have a sufficient vocabulary of adjectival descriptors, we should attempt to become engaged in this way of life. We should be able to describe what we see and feel – even if it is just to ourselves. If we can do this – understand the beauty and importance of what we are experiencing *as it happens* – we also can learn to become more engaged in those moments that do not occur as frequently. Becoming engaged in life as it unfolds in front of us is part and parcel of our story so far, anyway. We are there when it happens. We are enjoying the present moment and our history in the making. We are *engaged* in what it means to truly live, and not simply floating through existence transparently. We are *there*. We feel it.

There is another way we can actually attempt to *create* these moments. That is spontaneity. There is no guarantee that a beautifully simple moment will appear, but the mere fact you are doing something spontaneously increases those chances (it may also increase the chances of danger or insecurity or whatever else). The real loveliness of being spontaneous, however, lies in the fact that the nature of spontaneity itself is so simple. It requires no philosophy or forethought – indeed it spurns those things. Spur of the moment activity causes us to live with reactionary zeal, and appreciate the illustrious appeal of the present moment. The allure is in living for the sake of living, and not for the sake of anything in particular. This helps with the maintenance of our sanity now and all but assures it in the future, because it helps with the understanding of our control. It confronts head on our control issues and our proclivity for planning well into the chaos that planning itself causes. Consider chapter two and the idea of ultimate control. Ultimate control requires the understanding that we have much less control than we imagined possible ("gut hunch" alert!). It requires we acquiesce to the madness of this world – this absurd world spinning uncontrollably, with every conceivable catalyst working from diametrically different points of view. *This is our world.* We have no choice but to live in it. Being spontaneous helps us understand this more deeply; by definition, we have to "let go." It also makes life tremendously exciting because of variables unknown. Where will I end up today and whom will I meet? Variety and spontaneity are the spices of life. And the simple pleasures of life make each day a little less absurd and a little more worth the effort.

Part one of this book is now reaching its conclusion so let me take a few moments to summarize what I have essentially posited and explained. Although the philosophy may feel a bit scattered and is only loosely integrated, there is a running theme: all of the ideas presented in the chapters are subsumed within the idea of *engagement* and *immersion* in life. This, as I argued, is important for living a happier existence. Indeed, existing means nothing if we do not both choose for ourselves what it is to be, and do so with full clarity of action. And we cannot truly *exist* – much less enjoy some particular essence – if we do not come to terms with several things. These things I explained throughout this section, and I quickly review below.

We must retain our patience and control in the face of unending change and the vertigo-inducing fluctuation and inconstancy of life. We need to understand our place in the cosmos as unimportant, and the subsequent and attendant need to care for one another. Understanding what we really mean and think and say is an immeasurable attribute for clearing the bush and cobwebs of a confusing existence. Learning our history, as well as our connected stories, and sharing with each other our experiences and our help will lead to a meaningful survival in the few decades we have. Lastly, if we enjoy the simple passage of moments and life's simple pleasures – and become truly engaged in what it means for us to *be in* and *live* those moments – this life will have been far from squandered.

You may point out that this philosophy still leaves us with a sort of void to be filled with some kind of action. I think to some extent this is correct. This section was largely for how to think, as opposed to what to do. (Note that I suggest *how* to think and not *what* to think. And to the extent that it is actually *what* to think, it is only a suggestion. You can read this book, put it down, and forget everything; you have that right. These are observations that I have noted make the lives of people more enjoyable and meaningful – including myself. I can just hope you seriously consider the contents herein, because I do sincerely care about the outcome; this should be unsurprising when pondering my position on history and our connected existence.)

So what, then, of that void? This is the topic of the next section. I attempt to provide an explanation – replete with striking and expressive examples – for why pursuing art (in all its various forms and glory) can fill a void, or at least help maximize happiness and understanding in life. This will become much clearer in the next chapter.

You have your new wheels, and now you need some direction. An itinerary will be provided next. Do yourselves a favor and become the proverbial wanderer. Assume the roll of peripatetic lover of novelty. Join Whitman and Muir and Joni on the road to new discoveries and happiness. Take a chance, be spontaneous, and leap into something new and exciting. Expand your horizons, and watch your life blossom in front of your face. But do us both a favor. Do not forget to notice how you feel about it either.

PART 2

THE ARTS

CH. 12 WALKING THROUGH THE GATES

There appears to be in many of us some hole or missing link that is difficult to ascertain. At some point in time in our lives (usually at many times) we feel that our lives are not good enough, or that they are in some measure insufficient. This is a tricky feeling, because it may or may not indicate that a change is necessary. In many cases this is simply a case of human nature poking out its head. This is the existential unease to which I referred earlier in the book. If it is possible, while we still have breaths in our bodies, we typically yearn to achieve new things, to have what we do not have, and to push for the happiest and most fulfilled life attainable. This feeling will never subside, and nor should it. This pursuit is what keeps us alive.

The aforementioned feeling of existential unease could also mean that something particular *is* missing. However, if we are always searching and striving for new ideas and new forms of fulfillment, we will eventually achieve success in this pursuit. But as I said before, the feeling of never being satisfied is persistent and unalterable. Success, in this case, does not mean something static. How should we go about approaching this feeling? It is clear that something is in need of change – either something *actual* or simply our view of approaching and thinking about happiness.

As oversimplified and silly as it may seem, I categorize all persons into one of two main groups: persons living superficially and those living in the trenches. It is obvious at this point in the book that living "in the trenches" is the best way to live and the most exciting place to find oneself. It is almost impossible to climb back out of the trenches once there, but there is no reason to do that anyway. Indeed, you will find it hard to even conceive what it was like living on the "surface" in the first place. In using the term "trenches" I mean to signify a "deeper" understanding – and living – of life. No matter what we decide to do we should approach that with a deep care and interest in engaging and immersing ourselves with it. Why does that matter?

This matters because we are *missing all that is important* by not developing a *vested interest* in our activities. This section of the book is about how and why art - in a very broad sense - matters. You may not be missing a terrible amount by not really digging in philosophically to reality television programs, or the essential importance of fast food, say, or maybe what clothing is now in vogue. However, you would be remiss to let artistic pursuits scurry away unnoticed. Your mind is a sponge that will soak up about whatever you expose to it; if you are capable of achieving a deep understanding of various types of art – painting, music, photography, cooking, etc. – by simply *allowing* yourself to understand more about them, you will find your sense of excitement and purpose are almost uncontrollable.

It seems ludicrous to ask why excitement and purpose matter. For whom does excitement and purpose *not* imbue a consequent happiness? For whom do these things *not* translate directly into happiness? I submit that the people asking this are not sure what they mean by the word happiness. If happiness means anything, it is associated with excitement and purpose and love. These feelings can clearly be achieved with the simple pleasures of life, but to fully maximize these feelings – and your happiness – delving into one or several forms of art should be next on your bucket list.

I want to try one more way to convey to you, Dear Reader, the crisp distinction between living on the surface of life (knowingly or unknowingly), and being entrenched in life's beauties, subtleties, and fine details.

Imagine a majestic, massive gate standing in front of you. It is rather ostentatious looking, befitted with fine jewels and beautifully crafted lines and inscriptions, figures, and drawings (go ahead and throw in some ancient, arcane poetry). In other words, imagine something from an imaginative Hollywood movie. You already know that something worth seeking is on the other side of that gate. In a hypothetical film, typically only two scenarios exist: either the protagonist is meant to open and walk through the gate, seeking new wonders and adventures, or the gate represents something off-limits or untouchable. In the latter case, the protagonist opens it anyway and invariably walks through. There is something about that proverbial gate – that door of demarcation – that invites us to open it; it's something dangerous, something mysterious, something rewarding. In our case, we are not *meant* to open the door; we can choose whether we do or not. The door, however, (as we well know) has something intriguing, possibly life altering, on the other side. We reached out and turned the large handle with our philosophy. The door is now standing wide open with an iridescent display of splendid and palatial light pouring in on our side. We stand basking in the glow.

This section, then, is about making the decision to walk in, to cross the threshold from mediocrity, stagnancy and complacency to the marvel and grandeur of the other side. It is not always easy to understand things on the other side, but the adventures and struggles are always fun, and the rewards supply an almost unending excitement and sense of purpose. Becoming engaged on "the other side" – engaged in the arts of life – leads, therefore, to a happier existence. (If I am not defining happiness in the correct way, then I'm sure I have no idea what it means.)

I should mention what is not on the other side. There is no quick fix or instant version of life getting better. There is not some vision of the future or solid answers to the happiness question. I actually think most people would admit that happiness comes with the very struggle of trying to obtain it. Once we consider ourselves "completely happy" or "set for life," we have really already lost the battle for a meaningful existence. If the struggle for understanding or accomplishment means nothing, then the final outcome is, by definition at this point, pointless. The battle itself is fruitful; we bear the fruits of struggle, whether or not we achieve what we set out to do. What lies on the other side of the gate is the beginning of a journey (again, no Frost for you) for a meaningful struggle – a struggle for the understanding of the nuance and depth that art - and artistic pursuits - have to offer.

The arts – and, as we shall see in subsequent chapters, there are many examples of these – are worth exploring, because of the enrichment they add to our lives. The added enrichment comes from the depth of exploration available with these pursuits. The layers and nuance can keep us busy for long stretches of time, if not a lifetime. The alternative is to remain stagnant and to stultify our selves in such a way to render a completely unmemorable life, the decades passed and wasted by learning nothing new. Art would mean nothing if it did not allow us to explore such depths; indeed, the word itself would be meaningless. Imagine living a life where you could not understand – or would not want to understand – what excites other people. Or imagine a life where no one cared about what excited you. Understanding the depths of one another's passions can simply add more to our own plates. If *not* adding more passion or interest or excitement to our lives sounds like a *better* plan to you, then I will shrewdly point out I think you do not know what you're talking about. You may not know what full happiness is or have any real clue as to how to attain it. That's fair. But that was our problem in the first place, and if that is why you picked up this book then I suggest you at least give my recommendations a fair shot. It will pay dividends.

The next chapter jumps into what art actually is, and it attempts further to explain why it can be beneficial to your life. The following chapters, then, are particular examples of certain arts or artistic pursuits to consider. The ones discussed do not complete an exhaustive list by any stretch of the imagination. I just chose ones that I love, and they represent an interesting variety. You, Dear Reader, may partake in any art you deem interesting or inspiring. I only humbly provide examples. However, I provide a detailed analysis of why and how each art can affect our lives. Once you find your self ensconced in the steady pursuit of things artistic, it makes little to no sense to go back to zombieland. The philosophy is established, and we now have actions and adventures to fill the void. We are going to see an itinerary and many roads develop in front of our eyes. Our efforts at creativity and imagination constantly create new stretches of open road.

We have opened the gates. Now, look back behind you. What's there for you? The Hollywood film, at any rate, leaves no option. Let us take a chapter out of their book this time.

Walk through those gates.

CH. 13 ART: JUST WHAT THE HELL IS IT?

The last chapter was about making the conscious decision to pursue the arts wherever they might go. This will lead to a happier existence and fill the "void" left by our expelling the emptiness of a superficial life. In this life we have options about which avenues to explore, and we can assume any particular essence we like; we need to remember, though, that we exist first and can change our identities and interests if we choose. In this chapter I discuss the idea of art, what it is and what it means for us. This is the longest chapter and maybe the most contentious, but one that is necessary before we examine the particulars.

We all enjoy art to some degree. But we all seem to disagree on what art is. Is it a painting? Is it music? Can we consider a brilliant plate of food a piece of art? Or is cooking itself an artistic endeavor? Most people would certainly consider all the above as at least nominally artistic. But that very consideration raises important questions and criticisms. Who are we considering when we say "most people"? Can something "nominally" artistic really *be* artistic in any meaningful sense? And what, by the way, do we consider "brilliant"? That is surely a subjective term. As with most philosophical endeavors, we seem to fractionally enlarge our set of questions before we really even start. Such is the perpetual dilemma, I would argue, for any meaningful conversation. We have to define certain words in order to understand what we think about certain issues – to say nothing of what others may have to say about them.

I intend to issue some objective claims on what things we should consider as art. I also will argue that these "artistic" encounters or pursuits should be sought after to maximize our happiness (as I claimed in the last chapter). The goal here, then, is an attempt to cut down the excess brush that obfuscates our ability to truly -and objectively - appreciate art.

If there is one thing people don't like, it appears to be someone else encroaching upon their subjective sensibilities. They can like what they want and you can promptly go to hell. People are unrelentingly forward about their capacity to entertain subjective notions and, more importantly, the set of privileges associated with that capacity. I have noticed that even insinuating a possible objective method of obtaining happiness seems to appear an abrasive overstepping of social bounds. To speak normatively of happiness is to commit a grave sin. A typical conversation may unfold like this:

> X: I am going to an art exhibit tonight
> Y: I am going to the symphony this evening
> Z: You both have interesting evenings, but you *should* be coming with me to hear a talk on philosophy as part of a book tour. It is better for you. This will ultimately benefit you.

How can we make such claims? Aren't such claims grotesquely presumptuous at best, irredeemably intrusive at worst? Some individuals have surely lost friends because of such a conversation.

What if the conversation were framed differently? I do not mean by that an exposition or elaboration of their particular opinions. I mean to ask, what if the conversation were bound by different criteria? Consider the following conversation:

> X: I am going to an art exhibit tonight
>
> Y: I am staying in and watching a Jersey Shore marathon
>
> X: Really? Don't you think you could maximize your potential happiness by expanding your artistic horizons?

The immediate knee-jerk reaction by most of us would be to condemn Y while applauding and agreeing with X. However, that may only be because I framed the interaction is such a simplistic and dichotomized way. Upon further rumination, many would start to plug in more demanding questions. What if Y is truly happy watching a marathon of Jersey Shore? Furthermore, how could we actually *know* what makes Y (or anyone) happy? What about *truly* happy? ("I can truly like what I like, and you can truly go to hell.") Indeed, perhaps X only *pretends* to be happy by conforming to certain socially acceptable considerations of happiness. Perhaps X is swimming in a cauldron of self-deception or misconception. X believes that he is pushing his artistic limits and creating a perpetual atmosphere of intellectual and emotional stimulation. What if he is only fooling himself? Can we even tell if we are fooling *ourselves?* And even if we are relatively sure of ourselves, is it possible to discern this of others? If it *is* possible, there should be some objective criterion by which to do so. Perhaps more importantly, is it even worth our time? Why should we bother?

I do distinguish happiness from things like pleasure or enjoyment. I will expound upon that idea shortly. It is sufficient now to say that my conception of happiness is a larger and more permanent state than the latter two. We may *enjoy* many things that do not ultimately make us happy. A better heading for this chapter might have been, "The lost art of harnessing true happiness by pursuing artistic endeavors." But that isn't catchy. My authorial good sense would not allow that.

I asked if this endeavor was worth our time. I believe that it is not only worth our time, but so important that we should consistently reevaluate the specifics of art and why we should attain or study it. I also argue for the pursuance of artistic endeavors. I don't mean to split hairs, as they are both important and similar ideas. We may approach something in an artistic manner that may or may not itself be art – the study of history, say. What I mean by this is the full engagement or immersion in the subject matter. Both of these things allow plenty of room for growth and happiness.

Most of the aforementioned complaints, knee-jerk reactions, and numbing array of associated questions, converge into a simple linguistic concern. This is largely due to a definitional impasse. Once we define a few terms – or agree that we at least *need* to define a few terms – most of these complaints and questions fall away. I pay little heed to the notion that someone watching a Jersey Shore marathon could, with no prompting, philosophize their way out of a paper bag, much less into a conversation about happiness and art. However, *with* prompting they could – and that is important. I make no bones about this. We can answer many of these types of questions objectively, and I believe people can simply be wrong about being happy.

I'll repeat that last statement. I believe many people can simply be wrong about being happy. They can be under a grave misapprehension that they are happy or, in effect, pursuing happiness. This is not as far-fetched as it may initially seem.

Consider a drug addict and their daily routine. No one could reasonably deny his or her moment-to-moment pleasure or enjoyment. The anticipation of the ecstatic feelings and comfort - followed by those very feelings - could be some of the most pleasurable moments a person could achieve. Take a moment to imagine the mind of a serial murderer. The states of his brain while killing could be so spectacular as to render my trip to the museum embarrassingly dissatisfying. All sane people, though, would be quick to admonish the consideration of these pleasures as anything worth appreciating. We may appreciate the pleasures of getting drunk at New Years, and the thrill of driving home. We may also appreciate having sex eighteen hours a day (insofar as that's possible). We realize, however, that maximizing this notion of *happiness* encompasses a much broader, richer, and altogether different set of ideas. I do not want to switch my point entirely to the sole discussion of happiness, as the entire book hinges on and discusses this concept. I simply feel this is an important point to be aware of. If we can remain cognizant of this disparity, we can start to appreciate the arguments for objective methods of attaining happiness and growth. It is in this view that I now want to consider art.

Let us then return to art. There is a comically paradoxical line of reasoning when considering something as "art." Ask someone what he believes to be the main characteristic of art. Follow that question by asking him what one (any) characteristic of art is. The first is a broad question. The second question will often throw him into a frenzy of contradiction. The answer to the first question will inevitably be an attempt to broad stroke a definition of art. The need to do this makes perfect sense in light of our intuitions about these matters. What is the point of discussing art as anything interesting (or worth discussing) if we cannot talk about it objectively? However, the second question will often leave the person in paroxysms of postmodern backpedaling. In light of much of society being consumed in this whirlwind of relativity and liberalism, most people will quickly repudiate any form of blanket certainty. This is due in large part to religious absolutism (and its totalitarian underpinnings), and political and moral certitude. There is also a rich history of racism and sexism being conducted under the guise of objective claims (often touted as "science"... phrenology and social Darwinism to name just two egregious cases). People simply do not want to fall into a trap of foisting their beliefs and concerns on unsuspecting others. I think this notion is an important step forward for a viable global civilization. But, as with anything else, we have to continually analyze the pitfalls and encumbrances of certain ideas. I would do well not to find myself reproved after *any* objective claim into the moral sphere – to say nothing of other such slippery slopes like happiness or art. This, in my opinion, is a critical mistake; it is one that leaves us socially and emotionally impaired, if not altogether crippled.

This all leads us to an area between a rock and a hard place. I propose that art *has to have a definition*. That is the first point that others must concede. My definition – which I will give momentarily – may not be satisfactory to others. This is fine, and a discussion (or argument) over such a definition would be healthy and helpful. There has to be *some* definition, though, in order for art to mean something special. If art simply can be anything to anyone at anytime, then there is no point in discussing art. Art then becomes a meaningless word. Art now can be substituted with words like "paint" or "sounds" or "food." If *nothing* objective sets art apart from the quotidian drag of daily occurrences, and if *nothing* can improve our moral, intellectual, or emotional character, then here stops our discussion. We need not talk any further on the subject. If we can agree that there has to be some baseline proposal for differentiating art from non-art - as witnessed when others consider objectively the broad idea and merit of art - then we can start to have a productive conversation, and leave behind this inane (but well-meaning) sense that objective claims have no place in a subjective-oriented society.

I have a definition of art. I believe it to be hinged on the percipient (those perceiving or witnessing), and not on the "author." I would do best to give an example of what I mean. I spoke with an art student a few years ago (studying art at university level) that provoked me with an anecdote. She relayed to me that she had once seen a Jackson Pollock painting before realizing that it was a Pollock work. Indeed, she was not aware of Pollock at all. She admitted she thought the piece was "stupid," and did not think twice of it. However, one of her friends had apprised her of Pollock, his style, and about that specific work of "art." This is where the story gets interesting, and it is also where my incredulity started to raise flags. She then, apparently, as if in some miraculous moment of clarity, "understood" what was taking place. She understood – and not only that, appreciated – the work of "art" in question. Ostensibly, Pollock made perfect sense from that point on. This type of epiphany, in my opinion, is entirely predicated on the explanation of another, and is in no way some true moment of lucidity. If the author (or someone else) has to *tell you* it is art – and that you should appreciate it accordingly – it has lost the battle for recognition. There needs to be something recognizable about a piece of art, something that is recognized *as* art. The author of a painting or poem, the builder of a sculpture, the cook of an amazing meal, all have one thing in common: they need to be recognized by the percipient as having done something special. The key point to remember is the percipient need not *know* who painted or wrote or built. If a poem or piece of music immediately strikes you as profound, or a certain dish seems impeccable, it may very well be considered "art" by the producer of those things. Then again, it may not. But either way is beside the point. There has to be something else. There needs to be the recognition of *intent*. If a viewer sees intention – that is, they see an intention to create something specifically meaningful for others – then something can then be considered artistic. I also believe that some degree of formal skill is the next requisite consideration for designating something as art. I will touch more on that in a moment. I just want to point out that we can enjoy something that is not artistic (watching a sunset, playing Frisbee, or watching Duck Dynasty all day). Likewise, we may dislike something that we recognize as art. I may recognize the intent of a painting – a bucolic landscape, say – and still not care for it. Perhaps I do not like clear-cut lines or certain technical styles. Perhaps I like more abstract painting. But I have still recognized formal skill and intent. However, I recognize the author's intent to engage me for whatever reason. The only thing I need mention about formal skill is that it needs to be recognizable. If it even appears that a five-year-old could duplicate a painting, put together a structure (Legos), or produce a culinary dish (pb & j), it loses its artistic merit – or at least much of its luster and allure. This does not mean that simple things cannot be artistic; it just means there better be a hell of a lot of creativity behind something that requires no skill. Otherwise we simply have something that is cute, and perhaps likeable, but not something artistic.

In summation, I believe art is predicated on the percipient and not the author. Keep in mind that I argue that the piece does not necessarily have to be "moving" or "delightful" – indeed, one need not enjoy it at all – but rather that the percipient recognizes some form of intent (intent to move, intent to shock, or whatever).

There also has to be a level of formal skill involved. I take this to be self-explanatory. If I have assumed too much, I take the next section to answer some possible criticisms. Remember, though, that my first point of contention (it should not, as I hopefully have argued, be *that* contentious) was there needs to be some objective definition of art, some baseline on which the entire discussion is to rest. I certainly welcome a disagreement about what this definition could be.

I believe a section addressing criticisms is necessary. I think it is necessary not only here, but also for any argument where audacious claims are made. I should be able to foresee certain possible problems with my arguments. And there are some potential problems, as I already see it. I posit, however, that my arguments are not edgy or terribly controversial. They are (somewhat), in my view, philosophically uninteresting. My definition of art may spark some angry reactions, or at least some quizzical expressions. That, in my thorough view, would be about it. The only reason I would receive criticism – no matter how severe – (indeed, the only reason for developing these arguments at all) is because I am attempting to change the conversation. So what do I mean by that?

I really have only two arguments: a primary and secondary one. There may be confusion as to which is the more important one, so I will address these before I move forward. My secondary argument surrounds my particular *definition* of art. This argument matters, and it is important when considering my primary argument. However, my primary concern does not hinge in any serious sense on my secondary concern. As long as we can agree there needs be some definition we can soundly move forward. With my primary concern, I am arguing that *art is something that should matter to all of us* and *why* that is so. To make this argument, I had to develop a consistent *definition* of what art is –thus, my secondary argument.

Many of us share this intuition that art matters, and that everyone would be improved in some sense by engaging and appreciating it. But the "it" is what has remained an obstacle to this goal. This has gone unnoticed – or at any rate unaddressed - for too long. In our irrational fear of making objective claims, we effectively deny the ability for others to join the conversation; thus, the "others" don't ever realize their capability of appreciating art, and consequently maximizing their potential growth and happiness. My goal is to change this conversation. I needed to develop a thorough premise and thorough definitions in order to support my main goal. This is not just esoteric, philosophical huffing and puffing. The detractors, however, remain audible.

I can hear the vociferous opposition as I now write. "How can you ever say that one form of art is *better* than another? How can you suggest that a Rembrandt, say, is objectively 'better' than a Van Gogh?" This is a straw man, and I am not suggesting this line of argument. We can discuss the possible merits and demerits of each author, painter, photographer, chef and their specific works, without making an objective claim on one's superiority. I do not deny that this is *possible*, but it is not something in which I am interested (nor do I have a full conception of how this would be accomplished). My arguments are also not predicated on a comparative analysis between various *mediums* of art – photography and poetry, for example. I believe, while this may be difficult in practice, that it *could also* be accomplished in theory. Though I am not interested in this either. My *current* goal is to define what art actually *is*, and to objectively argue for its *capacity* to maximize personal growth and happiness. Developing arguments *between* different forms of art would generate interesting conversations. I believe this also to be a healthy line of thinking (much to the consternation of many art students), but this is, like I said, not my current objective.

Esoteric art aficionados discuss the beauty of art, both generally and particularly, on a regular basis. This is a useless exercise to the individuals who do not do this or know how this might be done. A much more important line of work would be to inculcate these "others" with a sense of art's objective, functional value. This is where the biggest – and, in my opinion, most unreflective – criticism of my arguments will occur; namely, telling others what they should appreciate. I need to take some time to address it. Before I do that, though, I need briefly to address some smaller, more specific criticisms concerning my secondary argument; that is, my particular definition of art. Once I have done that I will return to the bigger criticism. I will then hopefully have sufficiently addressed the necessary points of possible critique.

Any argument that inveighs against my objective definition of art is probably reducible to one main concern: that objective claims have no place in a subjective area of interest. Science, apparently, is the only value-free area where objective claims can be made with reasonable certainty. Suffice it to say, most people have a reflexive twitch when a seemingly value-laden subject – such as art - gets an obtrusive bump from an "intransigent" critic. I believe I effectively answered this criticism earlier and cleared up the confusion. I felt it important to reissue at this juncture. I mention it again because the real intransigence comes from the blind promulgation of subjective superiority over objective cluelessness. This is a problem. Everyone has an opinion, and they are certainly entitled to it. Where the critics are led astray is by the assumption that all opinions are all somehow right or correct too. All opinions are weighed equally in this light. This is such infantile, frightened capitulation. We cannot now know how art could be judged superior or inferior to other arts, or it would be next to impossible to adjudicate between art and non-art (and it would be next to impossible to discover). Just take a moment to fully imbibe and appreciate that thought. This is the sort of thing we regularly encounter. How could one ever say, for instance, that one subjective interest could be objectively better than another? This line of reasoning is itself aligned with an objective stubbornness; namely, that *we could never answer this type of problem.* Notice this also is only aligned with values *within* a decidedly artistic paradigm. These critics, you'll notice, would have no problem arguing that the person watching a Duck Dynasty marathon would be ultimately happier if they were participating in some form of art. They just say we cannot argue about art *itself.* I find this to be, if not a double standard, then a simple bait and switch. It is possible to never arrive at an answer to some of those debatable questions, but that does not mean there is not an objective answer to be found. We just need to agree on definitions. And, like I argued, the need for *some* definition is required if we are to make anything of "art."

Now, back to the "bigger" criticism. The critics of the bigger issue – critics of my arguing how one *should* spend their time – are a bit more unreflective, in a way. This is a deceptively easy criticism to answer. These critics would appear to have issued the ultimate *coup de grace* in subjective superiority. However, I don't think this is quite as sophisticated as they seem to believe. In fact, these critics may bypass the questioning altogether. "You can *never* tell someone," they might insist, "what they should do with their time, and what they should be interested in!" The real problem for the critics is with the word *"should."* One of my critics and I may agree that a better use of *our* time would be spending it at the Museum of Natural History. But my critic would balk at the notion that I suggest the couch potato (watching a *Honey Boo-Boo* marathon) *also spend time* at the museum. Now, if I merely suggest this as an option, it doesn't seem as coercive as *strongly* suggesting it. I find this a philosophically boring criticism. There is no real coercion. I am only finding objective benefits that the rest of us enjoy, defining and codifying them, and pointing this out to everyone else. I almost feel a social obligation to do this. They can, of course, take this information and simply choose to ignore it. I am not lobbying for new punitive laws that would incriminate the do-nothings or the cerebrally lazy.

Here is another specific example. The liberal relativist knows how to appreciate, say, a truly beautiful photograph. He would be at pains not to ponder it, perhaps discuss it in depth. He would even take the time to ensure his friends enjoyed it, as he would not want them to miss this opportunity for possible character growth. However, that is where his concept of ubiquity slams head first into his postmodern sensibilities. Suggesting to like-minded friends an artistic endeavor is perfectly normal, but to suggest it to another would be inappropriate, rude and pushy, or paternalistic. The mere use of the word *"should"* seems to metamorphose from one instance to another, and suddenly it is burdened with a coercive connotation. This is a painful and foolhardy extrapolation from one meaning to another. The obvious is lost in translation. The real condescension and paternalism wafts in on the breeze of separatism. "Well, *we* can understand and appreciate this meal, book, poem, and sculpture, but *they* cannot. They *need* those useless moments of pure vegetation to get by." They even recognize their hypocrisy when asked something like, "Do you feel that watching a marathon of E! News, listening to the Jonas Brothers, and stalking on Facebook all day can achieve any true, universal appeal for real growth and maturity? Is there something to be had there? Are we perilously and mistakenly turning a blind eye to something that can truly maximize our long-term happiness in this life? Are we missing something?" They know the answer to that question is an objective "NO." Yet they struggle with their verbal answer to this question. This timidity to speak truthfully, develop cogent definitions, accept and appreciate ubiquity in certain measures of happiness, and treat others with open hearts, is becoming a cancer on our collective interests. It reminds me of the atheists who offer this piece of unfortunate advice: "Well *we* know that there isn't any god, but *they* need it in their lives. They couldn't possibly get on without this idea, so you should not criticize their fairy-tale concept." I take the time to criticize, because I care about the answer. Imagine such a thing. I think the answer actually matters. Truth matters, and it is not subject to whim or fancy. People *can* be wrong about happiness and well-being. People *can* simply be unaware of the true possibilities of living a meaningful existence (as evidenced by the drug-addict, for example). I care enough to at least attempt my hand at these objective claims. If an individual subsequently chooses to ignore me, then obviously they have every right to do that. I am simply trying to issue a more useful and enlightening conversation.

The last question that may arise from a critic is one that is typically two-fold: "Let us say you are right, and we can – and *should* – speak objectively about art (and well-being and happiness, etc.). Why should we bother? What is so great and edifying about art or artistic pursuits?" They may follow that with the other part: "What if you do not convince them?" I have answered the latter question: you can only do what you can to present what you think will increase individual and even worldwide happiness. The first part of the question – as to why I bother at all - is what I will address in my last segment. This is the biggest question of all, and one that I have touched on throughout the last two chapters (and indirectly, but ultimately, throughout the entire book). The issue becomes this: what's all the fuss about?

Life for most people is a life of growing pains. We move through life enjoying pleasure and wincing at pain. We slowly start to realize that our happiness is dependent on some of those pleasures, and that it is forged through certain necessary moments of pain. We feel as if we can start to grasp "meaning" from that happiness. Then something else happens. We then begin to doubt that we ever had a good grasp on true happiness at all. This is the process of living. It does not end until it *ends*. So, all we can do is continually reevaluate what we can do to maximize that happiness. The process can have setbacks, but the notion of progress here is not just an illusion. We really do grow in terms of understanding our happiness. We really do learn what works best and what should be discarded. There are objective goals to reach for everyone. And, if we are honest, many roads begin to converge in this area. We all enjoy different things, and we all derive pleasure from different things; however, we – as human beings, sharing the same DNA and human condition – agree (socially *and* biologically) that happiness is achieved through a few basic core values. Not all of these values depend upon art. I stated this earlier. We all want to enjoy some sense pleasures – hiking, bungee jumping, water skiing, gazing at a sunset. We all want to be social in some degree – enjoying friends, a date with the wife, playing with the kids. We all enjoy when we achieve an intellectual or physical goal (whether or not we realized we should have actively pursued it). We strive to be altruistic. We empathize with our fellow creatures and help them accordingly. And we would be remiss not to notice the effect of that on our own happiness. However, we also realize that there is a balance to be had. We cannot physically or mentally withstand hedonistic pleasures indefinitely (hiking until we drop, sex eighteen hours a day, the solitude of a mountain journey, or defying sensibilities, fear and chance by jumping from a bridge loosely tethered to a bungee cord). Likewise, we cannot be around people all day (out with friends, all day with the wife, or playing with kids). We also cannot pursue intellectual and physical goals *ad nauseam*. As I previously mentioned, variety - as it turns out - actually *is* the spice of life. Though it is more than simply the spice of life. It is the means by which to maximize our happiness. We could not maximize our happiness by pursuing artistic endeavors for the rest of our lives. We would be missing too much the beauty and simplicity of simply enjoying the "moment" – quite literally, moment-to-moment pleasures (recall chapter eleven). Conversely, we could be happy for the rest of our lives by sitting on the front porch by a small pond in the mountains, and watching the dog and kids play in the front yard (sipping a cup of coffee, naturally). Though, in this case, we would not be *maximizing* our happiness because we would be ditching (knowingly or not) art and its benefits. Why we would we not want to maximize our happiness if we have control over it? We are not maximizing our pleasure or enjoyment in the attempt to eschew all possible painful experiences, but we are considering our happiness as the totality of our possible experiences here on Earth. When considering that, we should realize that we are not all so very different.

Pursuing artistic endeavors is actually more important than simply appreciating some piece of art. But, as I previously noted, that is not quite the design of this piece. I want to draw attention to the benefits of simply being able to notice and appreciate art. None of us enjoy every little thing that might be considered art. I noted this earlier as well. I also mean to say that we enjoy different mediums of art. Some may love painting and sculpture, and others may love cooking and photography. Still others may enjoy music and certain martial arts (the latter of which I consider to be more of an artistic *pursuit,* rather than something to *perceive*).

Learning to notice the intent, skill, and passion of others will help to add to your own happiness. When witnessing the intent and skill in a film - in everything from directing to acting to production - or smiling when understanding the meaning of a book – we should recognize that these are things that are uniquely human, and we are lucky to enjoy the capacity to appreciate them. What a waste of life it would be not to share in the passions of others. If we can recognize the passion and happiness of others like ourselves, we can do two things: we can appreciate what it is like to be or feel like someone else – someone who, with a few differentiating incidentals, could easily *be* us. The other thing is we also realize that we could add a new interest to this life – a life that only consists of a few short decades. There better be an afterlife for religious people, because ignoring these profound things only makes sense in light of an eternity – an eternity for a "do-over." (Indeed, the only reason I believe there is "ultimate" meaning in this life is because it does end…we have to get it right *in this moment*).

Imagine the fulfillment in simply recognizing the goals and passions of others. Others are attempting to bring together human beings in a shared experience, or they are sharing their take on what it means to live this life; one of which we are all a part. They are pushing themselves to their intellectual, emotional, and physical limits; they are sweating, bleeding, and crying over some pursuit of an ideal. This "something" is, of course, simply one aspect of this life. However, simply imagine ignoring these feats and accomplishments; imagine ignoring the attempt to push yourself and possibly explain or elucidate something more about this life and about being happy in this life. Imagine what it must be like to feel the sense of understanding and the sense of *otherness* that is possible. If we can simply *recognize* this intent and skill, it will improve us. We learn to not only enjoy it, but we also learn to ask our own questions. Hopefully, we gain the confidence to pursue similar endeavors ourselves. One can simply choose to "check out" of living in this sense, to skip the trenches and hold strong to the surface, but ask yourself why you would do this? What does one gain from such a move? What is the ratio of good to bad in terms of consequences? What is the point of diminishing returns? Anyone is capable of simply tuning in to this idea. That is why I feel it is important to spread the "good news" of art. I can speak objectively of how to live a life maximizing happiness (and what one should enjoy, in a broad sense), because it turns out that we are after the same things when stumbling upon real happiness. And, once again, it's possible to be unaware of what it means to be happy. A superficial happiness is meretricious and can be just as misleading. It isn't that I have some special ability to ascertain these things. I do not have doctorates, nor have I produced earthshattering displays of art. It just is not a required thing. We share this pursuit whether or not we realize it, and whether or not we realize *how* to pursue it. Our artistic interests may vary, but the notion of being interested and engaged in them absolutely should not.

The next chapters look at specific forms of art and provide reasons to possibly develop an interest in them. My goal with this is simply to give certain specifics of art, and why they each possess the depth of discovery that I mentioned could make a happy life more complete. You, Dear Reader, may do with these as you please. I suggest digging in to one or more, and watching how much more fun and consuming life will become. This particular chapter will make more sense as you read through the next chapters.

Hopefully, some of these artistic pursuits and hobbies will mean something to you and even change your life. If you are not already interested in them, just keep in mind this chapter's content about branching out and becoming absorbed in another's interest. These arts will help you connect with many others as well as with your self – the self you didn't know was there. Remember, also, that without caring to engage and to question, these arts become just mere superficial hobbies. They have the capacity to be so much more. And so do you. That is now up to you.

The room inside is capacious, so come on in and stay a while.

CH. 14 IN THROUGH THE LOOKING GLASS

> Photography is the gamut of feelings written on the
> human face, the beauty of the earth and the skies that
> man has inherited, and the wealth and confusion man has
> created. It is a major force in explaining man to man.
> – Edward Steichen

In Lewis Carroll's *Alice in Wonderland*, we see the "looking glass" representing a mirror that provides for Alice both clarity and an interesting (sideways) view of the world. Carroll probes into the depths of our imaginations for what is possible in a "mirror image," so to speak, of our world.

Our imaginations certainly are impressive, and although they get us in trouble sometimes they have lead not just to lovely fairy tales and good literature but also to some of our history's best inventions and most striking ingenuity. What about the world on the other side of the proverbial mirror? If we cannot have such fantastical things such as talking creatures at tea parties, is there then something else to be had? Can we learn anything from the analogy?

Consider a camera lens. Okay. Now consider our eyes. Our eyes of course were built from evolutionary pressure, and without jumping into that process (suffice it to say there is no "plan" or one-and-done attempt at the "perfect" eye[8]) it is important to point out that a camera lens is created through a much different process – a planned, perfected process. Our eyes see the world, but they do so imperfectly. Have you ever stopped to consider what we miss because our vision is flawed, or maybe because we simply are not paying due attention to our surroundings? Photography provides something different.

I'll not hasten to use the word "photography" just yet. Let's stick to the camera lens analogy. The near perfection of the image captured by great glass – found, say, on a nice Canon or Nikon camera (not to leave out the other competitors) – provides an astoundingly accurate view of the world surrounding us. So, while we do not see tea parties replete with odd, talking animals, we do see something of an interesting, unseen world – a world that is missed by our own imperfect eyes, which were crafted piecemeal via natural selection pressure. It is fun to ponder that our technology has created a device to capture the wonders of the natural world that our own naturally crafted units cannot truly and completely capture. That seems a quirky turn of events; but hey, that is why life is fundamentally cool and worth engaging in.

The technically crafted lens is capable of capturing a world that causes our own lens to widen in amazement and envy. This is seen with a wide variety of subjects or objects – a portrait of a beautiful woman, or someone languishing in poverty in a third world country. Perhaps we lower our jaw upon seeing the stark clarity of a city in the presence of a buzzing nightlife. A sly and understanding smile crosses our now roseate faces as we see a snapshot of the lights of the globe taken from remote space. In the same light we can become teary-eyed at a view of the natural word – a sunset over the ocean, or sunrise over the mountain, a

---

[8]   Richard Dawkins and other experts point out that the eye evolved independently at least forty times throughout animal history.

view of the trees, birds or other wildlife. With these images, we capture the absolute beauty as it stands then and there. And, as the world continues to spin interminably on its axis, there remains our perfect moment in time, captured through that perfect mirror with a singular click of the button. Sometimes the word beauty is hardly enough, overused as it is, to describe what we see. I would also add it is not quite apt to describe this process. Consider again the full process described. "Beauty" somehow pales in comparison.

The technical proficiency of a "photographer" is something impressive to behold. As I stated earlier, some requisite skill should be involved to consider something artistic. Indeed, many photographers do not like the term "photographer" anymore, because it is so heavily misused. According to them – and me – too many individuals are throwing around this term, calling themselves photographers when they do not deserve the title. That particular discussion, if I were up to the challenge in this book, would be long and involved. However, I want only to mention a couple of things on the matter. The reasons photographers should be considered artists are these: they possess the skill necessary in both "shooting," as well as editing and "producing" (and all of the endlessly associated technicalities), and they possess a well of creativity and imagination. They have acquired the skill, and have either acquired, developed, or – if you like – naturally possess enough creativity for the job. Some photographers are better than others (and the humble ones can easily admit this) because they have experience with the technical expertise, and have an endless well of creativity and novelty to be harnessed. The skill is not something I wish to dwell on for the remainder of this chapter. I do wish to further discuss the depths of creativity involved, and how it can affect our lives.

I did a colloquial interview with my friend, and budding new photographic talent in Nashville, Ramiah. Ramiah and I had a lovely discussion on photography that very naturally branched out into a larger, more inclusive discussion of art. As I suspected, he feels that the idea, value and merit of art is connected through all mediums or forums of it. Ramiah confessed to me that although photography was his current love and artistic companion, if he were to somehow lose this passion (or perhaps capability to shoot pictures for whatever reason) he would surely be involved in some other form of artistic pursuit. Photography, like all mediums of expressing our selves to the world, allows for us to grow and share with one another. We share happiness, sadness, confusion, despair, friskiness, wisdom, etc. This is why it matters *as* art; we can explain our selves to the world and we can explain our selves to our *selves*.

Ramiah is also a guitarist. (This was our initial interest in one another. We shared a college major in Exercise Science, but we found that we both loved the Blues. I discovered he loved and played Jimi Hendrix and SRV and BB King and on and on. We also share an almost unhealthy musical obsession with John Mayer. Once I uncovered his predilection for music, I knew he would be involved in something else artistic. He was not a photographer at the time.) Although Ramiah and I agreed on the point about always pursuing some form of art and "once an artist, always an artist," he also, to my pleasant surprise, agreed with my conception of existence preceding essence. He admitted that he might not be in love with photography one day, but that no matter where his life led he would be in search of something bigger, something deeper, and something that "explained" life or made life a little more pleasant. This, brothers and sisters, friends and comrades, is why art matters. Photography is just one way to dig your self into the trenches.

That perfectly crafted lens does not do all of the work. At this juncture, technical skill rolls into creativity or imagination. We are still capturing the real world, but we are doing so with an unmatched precision and an "eye" for the "magical."

Sometimes words just cannot do an instance justice. I consider myself a good writer, and pride myself on describing things with a keen eye and with assiduous detail. It is evident though that in many cases one needs a picture to do a moment justice in capturing the right feelings - a picture may be worth a thousand words, more or less, but the point is moot. The irony is hard to miss, here. I, using this medium, can only *write* to explain the sheer magnificence that a single picture can emote. I trust, though, that much of my readership knows what I mean. Many of you reading this have seen a picture that has changed you to some extent, even if only momentarily. I could write the entire day and sedulously (and with much pain) describe the richness and dazzle of just one picture of a single tree, and it would not touch a great picture of that tree. Although most of us have been impressed with a picture at some point in our recent lives, many of us do not think any further on the artistic grandeur of photography.

Not all of us should use the term "photographer" when describing ourselves, but I would rather that be the obnoxious epidemic than the alternative; that is to say, no one considers photography as anything worth pursuing. Recall what I said earlier about caring about others' passions. Allow yourself to become immersed in the "art" of another. In this short life, it is possible to grow and evolve by becoming engaged – engaged in everything, including arts. Photography, like other arts, allows us to fall so deeply into the details and nuance (indeed, it possesses the capacity for details and nuance) of its hills and valleys. When looking to capture a moment or to capture a particular *feeling*, all of our senses have to be heightened and in full force. This, by definition, is being engaged. To create something that means anything lasting and monumental for you and for others, you have to care enough to be engaged.

If we become engaged and immersed in capturing a moment in this world, we can truly "see" what is out there for us to see – both in the sense that the lens is more exacting, and in the fact that we are *looking* for the world around us. We are *looking* for that perfect shot. We are astutely screening an individual to capture that face, or that feeling that encapsulates what we want to convey; what we *need* to convey, or sometimes, what we did not even realize we wanted to convey until the perfect moment presented itself! We are fastidiously combing mental and emotional checkpoints in order to snap that perfect picture of the dreamy sun disappearing behind that unreachable horizon. We begin to realize there is an endless array of moments in this world to "capture." From that realization comes an inexhaustible search for what life has to offer, a search for the moments in between and the moments that fall away unnoticed. In short, we learn to become engaged in art and in life. We are then always engaged, even if we are not holding a camera. This is the beauty and art of photography. It can easily be a gateway to a better and more discerning life – both ideologically and in all the real moments that we capture as they proudly and gorgeously stand.

Ramiah had somewhat of an inauspicious beginning as a "photographer." As is the case most of the time with most people with almost any new interest, there was no immediate spark that allowed for him to miraculously hone his craft. It took time to develop skill and interest. The riveting thing is that skill and interest grow over time and can be sustained indefinitely. Especially the interest and passion, as that can be a motivating factor for a lifetime. He developed an increasingly engrossing interest, and every day honed and crafted this hobby. He takes seriously the ceaseless depths of this art, and he prides himself on his humility in understanding how long and arduous the journey is to greatness. He understands his place in the pantheon of greats, and he recognizes how much room there is to grow. Ramiah also loves what comes with his particular niche of photography: people. He loves to meet new people from different backgrounds, and he loves to socialize with them. These experiences would only be amplified with a photographer who traveled the globe. As you see, the associated experiences with being a photographer - as we hear from Ramiah and many others - also have their merits and are worth noting.

The good thing about having artistic friends is the ability to have seemingly everlasting conversations. Sure, we can get together with our guitars and play "Every Day I Have the Blues" (and contort our faces accordingly) but we can also fluidly develop a conversation about the artwork of an album - be it picture, drawing or painting – and continue our time together well into the night. If you have ever been around someone for whom conversation seems a terribly painful or difficult experience, then you appreciate much more the friends with artistic interests. They understand the depth of art and the subsequent depth of life.

Deciding to jump in through the looking glass is a decision to notice life more intently. You can watch the interest in life develop right in front of your own impressive, but evolutionarily flawed eyes[9]. The lens is a magnifying glass for the world and for the meaning of your own life. The difference in Lewis Carroll's version and our own is that his mirror created a new existence. It

---

[9] Really, our human eyes are hardly worth writing home about. There are more productive and impressive eyes out there. Any serious study of the eye will show you what I mean.

is fair to say that the art of photography can create a new existence for our lives. The life magnified by *our* looking glass, however, is not a fabricated one, but instead is the real thing. We see it in all its majesty and ruin. We recognize that *this* is the world in which we live. We capture it as it truly is. And we capture our selves in the process.

CH. 15 SAVOR THE BITE

I can't stand people who do not take food seriously
– Oscar Wilde

You have to be a romantic to invest yourself,
your money, and your time in cheese
– Anthony Bourdain

A bottle of red, a bottle of white, it all
depends upon your appetite
I'll meet you any time you want, at our Italian restaurant
– Billy Joel

You are on a cruise. Experiencing all things involved in such an environment helps you lose yourself in a fantasy where your problems seem not to exist. The boat is massive, the décor is gorgeous, and the service is perfect. The experience is unrivaled. The deck is open and spacious, the people are happy and enjoying themselves, and the food is sumptuous and decadent. These will be some of the best memories you will acquire. You take it all in.

This type of experience is easy to understand if you have ever been on a cruise. Every experience is accepted with alacrity, and we seem to understand that we should be engaged with every possible one. We appreciate the special, brief nature of this "vacation," and adjust our feelings and emotions accordingly.

My contention from the beginning is that we can have these experiences everyday in many different scenarios – even seemingly "mundane" scenarios. This does not denature or devalue the experience of the cruise; the cruise is just one more spectacular experience to relish. Great experiences also necessarily lie on a gradient or continuum. Some are better than others for certain reasons, and the cruise may very well be one of the best. The feelings of savoring a sunset or vast, blue ocean are carried all the time. We are usually aware of those things. There is, though, typically one aspect of a cruise that seems to be underappreciated when not cruising: the food. Why a sunset but not food? Let us take a look into this.

This chapter is about savoring the bite: figuratively and literally. Food and cooking are arts that are often forgotten or simply overlooked by the majority of non-chefs. It is easy to overlook how food and cooking can help us engage in life; it is easy because food is all around us and we do not have time to think about it – we just eat it. Fast food and frozen foods allow us to make ingesting "nourishment" (nourish yourself with this delectable chicken Mcnugget) an extremely small part of the day. It doesn't have to be – and shouldn't be – this way. We are forgetting about all of these arts in which we can become engaged because, if you recall in part one, we fill our day with any and everything possible, forget about time as something precious, and never actually stop to smell the roses. We should stop and smell the aroma of food once in a while, too. I believe our lives can be improved by doing so.

Just like with other forms of art, we have here both the requisite depth (the trenches) to dig into our creative reserves for a nearly a lifetime, and we have the ability to develop a technical skillset as well. Okay, so we have the essentials to make "art." So what?

Why is food and cooking such a big deal? Well, it does not have to be a *big deal*. Every person has to choose which art they wish to "try out" or in which to become engaged (if any). Perhaps understanding food and the art of cooking is not high on your list. But I will provide reasons to consider it. It happens to be one of my favorites, and is something to which I aspire further in regards to skill, creativity and understanding.

Orson Welles once quipped, "My doctor told me to stop having intimate dinners for four unless there are three other people." This is something with which many people can relate. Here in America where I am writing this book, many Americans have a love-hate relationship with food. We love to eat, and hate to be fat (and subsequently convince ourselves it's ok with pick-me-ups like: "I'm big and beautiful!" and "I love myself, and you are just jealous!") This, however, is not the relationship I speak of. I speak about cooking and food as an art form, as something that can improve and enrich our lives. It does so in a few ways.

"In France, cooking is a serious art form and a national sport." This is a quote from renowned chef and interesting entertainer, Julia Childs. History and competition are indeed two of the ways this form of art can improve our lives. There is a rich history of cooking and dining and preparing certain foods, and there is obviously a much richer history and science to food itself. The history and science behind foods could occupy our time until our dying day, and that is only part of the fun and the depth of artistry. The competition among foodies and chefs and other perfectionists is another enriching aspect of this engagement. Competition is usually healthy, especially competition among ourselves. Striving to become a better you, in all respects, seems to have no viable alternative in regards to living a happy life. Who wants to settle with mediocrity? Defining goals and yearning to become a better chef, or more knowledgeable about food than you were yesterday, is a steady and sure way to never become bored with life.

Another way studying and understanding food is enriching is because of the depth in such knowledge and creativity. The creative outlet and utility of preparing dishes is full of variables. For instance, what "style" do you have? Are you about French technique and classical arrangements? Are you a spicy, Spanish-inspired chef? Or are you maybe a hearty American mélange? Within that paradigmatic view, what nuances make your food special? This type of open road allows you to discover yourself in an ongoing process, to say nothing of interacting with others and helping them get to know themselves. The nuances in the culinary world are very particular. Anytime that is the case, you can expect divergence and creativity and competition. For instance, do you have technical grasp and understanding of terms like "julienne" or "au gratin"? Would you be able to make or enjoy a paprika emulsion? Could you tell if your food had hints of coriander?

You, Dear Reader, may think I am getting a bit too fancy. Who cares about hints of coriander? If the food is good, it's good! Well, true enough I suppose. But *why* is the food good? What does *good* even mean? If you are not able to understand why the food is "good," then you will not be able to reproduce such food or even ask for it again in the future. So, one element here is understanding what you enjoy and why you enjoy it. Another element is having this understanding form a common ground with other individuals. Sharing a love for food and cooking, just like any artistic passion, can lead to friendships with others who also share and understand the same things. Through growth and patience we can dig through the beautiful trenches of this art, and add a new spark to our lives – including the spark of new relationships.

The culinary arts, along with helping develop new social relationships (we saw the same with photography) and a development of self-confidence and approval, also provide ancillary interests. Gardening and outdoors healthy living (and general green-thumbery) can provide an additional patience and growth, the likes of which I discussed in chapter ten, on or about nature. "Field-to-table" service is part and parcel to becoming more *physically* healthy as well. Those are just some of the associated interests with which to become involved. And those interests in turn open new vistas of opportunity for growth and happiness. The world just seems to get smaller as I write – in a good way.

From cultural understanding and interest, to self-empowerment and adaptation, the culinary arts leave a big imprint on our lives. This is not more important than other arts; it is just an example of an art that can do what all good art can: provide a context and platform to discover more about yourself and about others. Cooking is something that takes patience and skill, and an appreciation for nuance and subtlety – add to the mixture a healthy dose of spontaneity and playfulness. We do not have to be fancy French chefs, but – like all other arts – becoming engaged, and even entrenched, in the all-encompassing details of this art, will leave us better off as people. We can understand different cultures, different attitudes and proclivities for tastes, and we can help define or broaden our own limits in life. A quote I like from an internationally known chef, Justin Quek, reminds me of this book's take on a healthy life, and transcends mere cooking. "When you're eating something and your palate tells you something is missing, that's when you start combining." Indeed. Life works the same way. Become playful, learn new skills, and above all, become engaged. When something is missing, go ahead and start combining… and be sure in the process, comrades, to savor the bites.

CH. 16 CANVASSING THE HEART

Painting is silent poetry, and poetry is painting that speaks
– Plutarch

Painting is just another way of keeping a diary
– Picasso

Imagine you are reading a book. Bear with me. Assuming you are engaged in the book, your mind will create imagery for the story. The author may do a fine job of setting up a scene or a character with a strong adjectival command. Ultimately, though, the imagery conjured is as vivid as you make it. You, as readers, take the text and transcend it; you transcend mere words and conjure up pictures and sounds and colors – you bring life to the text. One aspect of this – the "pictures" - can genuinely help elevate a text. (The "sounds" element of this will be the addressed in chapter eighteen.) What if we consider the reverse scenario? If we look at a painting, can we see life happening in words and sounds?

The focus of this chapter is to consider the art of painting; although, I hasten to point out while I omit "drawing" or "stenciling" or even charcoal work, I certainly include those arts in this general category of visual art. Painting encompasses a very elaborate and often heart wrenching - in both good and bad uses of the term

- set of artistic technical devices as well as emotions. As much as photography captures the "real" world in a specific moment – and as much as that is beautiful – a painting can capture something different. A painting can capture another mirror of the world as we see it. If photography is the mirror to the world, then painting is a mirror to the mirror – it is filtered through us first, and not an exquisitely crafted lens. In this case our minds are the lenses, and in this case we are "onto the canvas" as opposed to the "in through looking glass." And to get there we first have to journey once again through the confines of our minds. First stop: Creativity town on the corner of Engaged avenue.

A spark not just of creativity, but also of *life*, is needed to paint anything worth seeing. So, who gets to be the judge of what is worth seeing? If you recall, I addressed that as best I could in chapter thirteen. I won't rehash that now, but I will remind the reader that intent and some form of technical skill must be involved and, most importantly, recognized. This spark is an interesting and endearing one because it includes not just a technical set of skills and initial engagement, but also a secondary filtering process. What do I mean? A photographer has to be ready in the moment, but once the shot is done there can be no tampering or fixing it (this can be done in post-shot editing, but this is a different concept). A painter has to take the concept from an image or idea, and then go through the process of developing what she wants in entirety. In other words, it cannot just be a finger-to-button process – there are two large steps instead of one.

The painter, in this two-part process, may change her mind about the direction of the painting, or even the idea itself. This is where painting becomes an artistic process. One of the main areas of artistic nuance is the process of error correction. It is obviously very easy to make a mistake in the process of completing a painting, from idea to finished product. The more technical the painting – or the more "difficult" or abstract the conception – the more room there is for error, one way or another. This capacity for error gives the artist the necessary wiggle-space to express herself *as* an artist. Perhaps the colors she mixed are not "working," but instead of starting over on a clean canvas she simply transitions, transposes or maneuvers her way around this issue. Perhaps her entire idea changes. Not simply giving up or even starting over, she shows herself adept at being creative and thinking on her feet. This form of mental acuity is impressive, and coercing ourselves to do such things would, I'm sure, improve our mental capacities. However, there is more than meets the eye with this canvas of information.

Let us consider the other side of this art: appreciating and understanding artwork (as opposed to creating it). What would it mean to "get it" when witnessing a painting? What would it mean *feel* it, to get emotionally involved? Would we even have a choice in doing so? Would it not just "happen"? For many paintings (as with other art forms) we would simply and involuntarily "get it." Though I believe that speaks not just to the author's abilities, but also something innate in all human beings: this capacity to understand the human condition, and our capacity for appreciating and relishing the transcendent. The human condition is rife with every conceivable emotional disposition, and a painting can touch one, many, or even all of these – even with the same piece!

Conversely, if we do not necessarily "get it" when looking at most works of art, it does not mean we lack the human capacity to appreciate our condition; indeed, learning to *awaken* to the emotional power and knowledge around us is our *human story*. We are the cosmos finally come to know itself (we are, in Sagan's term, "stardust"). Much like how we appreciate the scientific fact that we awoke from a cognitive slumber, became curious, and eventually developed culture; we also can learn to awaken to see the human spirit in paintings...and in everything else. What we create, in these senses, *is us*.

Consider how ideas change and how that affects the technical and creative aspects of art in paintings. In Renaissance Italy the cultural efflorescence that took place (with the serendipitous event of many artistic geniuses being in the right place and born at the right time) allowed the Florentine paragons of art to achieve dizzying new heights. They also broke new barriers. Artists like Brunelleschi, Donatello, Ghiberti, Boccaccio, and Michelangelo proved iconoclasts in areas such as building, sculpting, writing, and painting. In high Renaissance painting, new ideas (or old ones revamped) about the human condition as it related to itself (humanism), as well as technical breakthroughs (vanishing points, foreshortening, and general perspective techniques), pushed the ability to understand their technical and creative capabilities.

Consider what paintings "had to say" about social or political life. Consider what it says about simplicity. Looking at "Starry Night" (Van Gogh), one may cull a simple beauty from the visual, although, if one wanted, there is much more to learn about the technique, as well as philosophical underpinnings. Take a moment to take in Grant Wood's famous "American Gothic" piece. This piece is now one of the most iconic - and lampooned - works of art available. What does it say about our slice of Americana? Who are we as people? What do we appear to be to others? Hell, what are we doing with our lives?! These questions and more can be asked of a single painting; an image that is both considered heavy artistic cargo, and prime material for parody or satire. It might as well be holding up a sign that says, "I'm art! Check me out!"

Personally the impressionists, like Monet, give me pause for reflection. The technical style of blending colors and the use of quick brush strokes allow for an altogether transcendent experience. This technique and creativity can display life almost as it is - using colors, for instance, to represent a *very* specific time and type of day - while simultaneously distorting it in almost cartoonish fashion. A work of Monet (pick any you like) can appear like a work of stained glass. The fact this is possible already motivates me to understand more about life and its human displays and representations; it keeps me engaged in both the process and the final result.

John Atkinson Grimshaw is arguably my favorite painter (arguing with myself, that is). Just you look, Dear Reader, at "Boar Lane, Leeds, by Lamplight," "Greenock Dock," or "Lights in the Harbour." Mediate momentarily on his "Meditation," "Nightfall Down the Thames," or "October Gold" (which is *haunting* and tear-jerkingly moving). Grimshaw's work shows people and objects in the world; he paints these subjects, and objects, as they would appear from afar. He does this as if to say, *"this is exactly how the world looks at this moment with no variation."* Yet he does this with oil and paint, and not with a camera. He also does this while distorting the clarity as if to say, *"we can never live up to this moment, we can never relive what we've done, and all of this life is but a hazy blur as we spin on this axis."* This is what I get out of his work, and this is why it moves me.

This is why painting can help us reach unforeseen depths, and one of the many reasons we can use it to enrich our lives. I ask you just to find an artist, or even just a painting, that can make your life stop for a few short moments. From there will grow an insatiable appetite for the wonders of the brush and for the sparkle of colors. For this brush and these colors can be the vehicle to add so much new color to your own life. Take an idea like a spark to a flame; the idea is the kindling, the colors and style are your flame.

The canvas will then be your eternal flame. And just like Prometheus, you take your fire and start your life – throwing wood on the fire until there are no more logs to burn…or until the sun comes up.

CH. 17 ROLL WITH THE PUNCHES

Jiu-Jitsu is like a philosophy. It helps me learn how to face life
– Helio Gracie

Now that we have peeked at some calmer arts, let us look now to something a bit more physical. Brazilian Jiu-Jitsu has been an interesting thing for me, because it embodies both the physical and mental aspects of art. Considering a martial art an actual "art" may sound strange (even though "art" is right there in the name) and, in many cases, there is less "art" than practitioners would have you believe. Jiu-Jitsu is an altogether different animal, and it has added much to my own life in the way of patience and control, both physical and mental. Take a moment, Dear Reader, to see why this sport is much more than what it may seem.

The main thing that makes Brazilian Jiu-Jitsu (Bjj) special and at least worth noting is its majestic simultaneity. There is more than that, but that is the main thing. Its tremendously rare simultaneity renders it beautiful both in practice and in theory. So, what are we talking about, you ask? On the one hand, we are physically stimulated and possess a dangerous, martial skillset, and on the other hand, we are eschewing altogether the very nature of physically domineering masculinity. We who practice it can both cause physical damage, and (or) we can learn to simply let go of our egoistic view of the universe – to transcend the concept of self. Sound completely odd? It is. The interesting thing, of course, is that we *have* that option *at all*. How could we be talking about the same thing? In one view, we are being physically stimulated, protecting ourselves, and adding potent fuel to our testosterone-driven fire, and when looked at with a different pair of goggles, we see that we can be more gentle, caring, and passive than we ever imagined we could be. If that isn't an interesting dichotomy I don't know what is.

I want to start with the physical attributes of Bjj. From a physical perspective – which may be all that neophytes notice – the allure of Bjj is one of calculated dominance. When honestly mulled over, most people realize a "grappler" – and his skillset – is realistically a more dangerous opponent than anyone else. Perhaps "dangerous," in the acute sense, is a misnomer. A good kicker may inflict more damage than would someone performing a double-leg takedown. But the winner of the fight is usually the one that dictates that fight. The grappler has complete control when the striker is off his feet. In that sense, then, the grappler possesses a much wider array of realistic skills being utilized in more realistic circumstances. There are also an almost infinite variety of skills to employ with Bjj. There are only so many punches and kicks for a striker to throw. My mentioning these facts is not to comparatively denigrate other martial arts, but only to display the appeal of Bjj. There are other physical benefits as well.

Try punching and kicking each other in the head - at near one hundred percent capacity – for long stretches of time. Your health would quickly deteriorate. This is not something with which Bjj practitioners are concerned. The "light" nature of the mechanics while sparring (or even competing) allow for full engagement, while still minimizing serious danger or concern. Something else to add to this great fact is that this form of physical exercise – or, if you like, self-defense – can be developed and employed into the "golden" years; in other words, you can still do it when you are old. The joints, muscles, and bones hold up relatively well in Bjj. So, considering only the *physical* nature of it we see the glaring benefits. It is the most "dangerous," in both the sense that it is pragmatic or aligned to realistic situations, and that the depth and variety of the skills is so impressive. It is also the safest in that it allows for relatively safe practice at close to any age. Both of those things are almost contradictions in turn. And we haven't even reached the mental and emotional benefits of this Gentle Art (a term which I will examine at the end).

The mental enticement or charm of Bjj is, in my opinion, more gratifying than its physical merits. This aspect is not usually known before getting into Bjj. It is experienced. If you like: the physical brings them in – the mental makes them stay. So, what do I mean by that? What was all that fluff I mentioned earlier about caring, and losing the ego, and relaxation, and wakefulness, and rising above the self? That sounds as contraindicative as it could be considering what an amazing physical set of rewards is provided by this very same activity. What gives? What gives is the majesty of this particularly special dichotomy. It is this majestic simultaneity I spoke of at the beginning. While it is true to say this self-defense or sport can be dangerous and physically domineering, it is just as true to speak of the mental acuity necessary to play the game. It is very much like a game of chess between opponents. The goal is to win a strategic victory. The difference is in Bjj there are a hundred ways to get to the finish line, many of which your opponent will never see. In chess your opponent can at least see the board. In Bjj you are blind to the board while you try to stay as many steps ahead as possible. That certainly makes for at least an intriguing, if not an exciting, match.

During the crafting of your mental acuity and the harnessing of your physical acumen, you develop also a passion for your opponents - now and in futurity. I mean to say that both people develop a respect for each other. However, it is more than just a respect. It is a quiet understanding of the human condition, the fallibility of humans, and our physical, mental, and emotional shortcomings. It speaks to our fears, our weaknesses, our strengths, and our concerns. This point is where the caring comes into effect. This is where you start to lose the ability to see things from a completely solipsistic point of view. It is no longer about you, or even your opponent. It is about seeing people as they truly are: human beings who are happy, sad, and strong, weak, scared, and courageous, confident and confused. No one beats the odds of fallibility. No one gets a pass on feeling the pangs of defeat. The strongest of wills and most confident of minds will be put into a "triangle" or "armbar." The sense of self that walks onto the mat is transformed by the time it walks off. That sense of self is knocked down a few notches (maybe more) once you practice this art. You feel the helpless and ineradicable feeling of drowning. But each new day of practice shows that you can learn to swim as you proceed. Each new day provides a window of opportunity for personal growth, and a window to see the rest of the world more clearly – a world where *you* are not front and center. Need I chirp about the benefits of this?

Lastly, I want to mention something about "letting go." This is an important concept in life, especially if you wish to make it through relatively unscathed. There is a practice in Bjj called "flow rolling." During this process, the "opponents" (friends rolling with each other) let their muscles – in body *and* mind – simply disappear. You will willingly concede a position simply to discover where you will arrive next. This is much more philosophically robust than one might think. Consider the implications and analogies.

Our sense of confidence as humans is built around control – control of our actions and abilities, and the control of how we feel about them. In the dark is obviously what we cannot see. The dark is around the corner and is too demanding of our control. Do you attempt new activities in your life? Do you travel unknown avenues to see where they might lead? Can we, as fallible humans, accept the responsibility, excitement, and fear of letting ourselves go long enough to find ourselves all over again? Or maybe we just find someone new? Think about that. That is what it is like "flow rolling." I let my ego disappear. I give up my control only to find myself again. I relinquish my control, and simply melt away in the moment. I become satisfied with the moment. This appears to be a running theme. I can think of little else more rewarding.

Is it any wonder how we, who practice this, become so attached to this sport – this lifestyle? It is more personally rewarding than many other things because of its rare dichotomy. We are all physically and mentally rewarded, and we learn to live comfortably with others and with ourselves. We come to understand each other as human beings - and all that is associated with that - and we learn to grow and to help others grow, on *and off* the mat. Should Bjj be given the sobriquet, "The Gentle Art?" I don't know. Perhaps, "Gentle attack" or "Gentle self-defense" would be more apt. I do not know of any art form that is intrinsically *not* gentle. That seems a silly descriptor. Bjj is of course artistic, and it can certainly be gentle. But, in my opinion, any such short description of the sport does a bit of an injustice to all that it ultimately entails. It is something that needs to be experienced. And most can reasonably count on becoming better for it.

I included this particular art to throw a wrench in your idea of what art might consist in. Half of the battle concerned in this book is learning to recognize, or even seek out, ways to engage in this ephemeral life. You now see that even something as physically demanding as Brazilian Jiu-Jitsu can be as artistic as painting or cooking or performing music. Hopefully, Dear Reader (now I may call you Dear Roller), you will understand that Bjj can help you learn to roll with the punches, both on and off the mat. The trenches are there, and they provide so many riches for your life: patience, control, care, humility, understanding, empathy, and health benefits. As always, those riches can be shared with others to help improve their lives as well.

CH. 18 STRIKE A CHORD FOR HARMONY

> Without music, life would be a mistake
> – Nietzsche

> After silence, that which comes closest to
> expressing the inexpressible is music
> – Aldous Huxley

The last foray into the land of the arts concerns music. Music is something that touches everyone in every culture. This is one of the most obvious "arts" and one that most can easily enjoy. There is something special and unique about the emotion that music inspires. It is so easy to succumb to, or find yourself immersed in, some theme, some instrument, or even just a sea of sounds. Although music is easily agreed upon as an important art, I just wanted to add a few more points to finish a very short – and in some ways perfunctory and unjust - chapter on the subject. (Because of its universality and ubiquity, music does not require a remaking of the wheel in terms of explicating its importance. I just add a few additional observations.)

Music is not just a good escape from the daily drag, or something that makes you feel good. It has the ability to do two special things. The first special thing is it can immediately vaporize your connection with reality. This can be a bad thing in certain circumstances (driving at night, say, or directly before a job interview). One of the important things about art is that it provides this disconnect from reality. This is important for all of us to have, because it keeps us playful, creative, and alive into old age. Music can help achieve this state almost instantly. I will not bother trying to use my words to describe this feeling that occurs with sounds. Forget the lyrics (I would include those with poetry or literature); the *sounds* are what come together and, sometimes within seconds, whisk us away from reality and any attendant problem we may have. This leads to the other special thing about music.

Unlike other art forms, the nature of this medium is so strange and malleable. All of the other arts can stimulate a visceral reaction, but we are witnessing or tasting something in those scenarios. Music allows for a culmination of the other arts. Hearing sounds can immediately draw pictures and tastes and colors. The pits can abruptly drop from our stomachs, or the tears yanked from our eyes. It is an exceptional biological and physical process. Hearing sounds, vibrations in your ear that get converted in your brain, can and do provide such profound moments of ecstasy. Put aside pop music for a moment (with the sweet memory of you and your boyfriend's first kiss) and think about the droning and rhythmic chanting of some special rite or event for Hindus or Africans, or even monks. The entire lives of some of these peoples can be devoted to something involving sounds (not even "music" as we would consider it). But even considering the wide variety of music and its effects, we can all see clearly that all types of music affect us differently. Something about it as a whole can either take us to the stars or tear us apart – and can do everything in between. We cannot take that lightly. Why would we want to?

In music we see ourselves, and we see everything we never knew we were or could be. We see in ourselves and in others the ability to understand each other with no words. Music is sort of a universal language in this respect. In an instant certain sounds can change your mood, if not seemingly your entire life. And with music harmony is just mathematical. All of this love and care and concern and every other emotion are dictated by a calculated change in harmonic or melodic notes. It's that simple. Try adding a major seventh note to your vanilla major triad, and watch your *mood* change. Add a "second" note on top of that to produce a "maj9" chord. Now you are playing jazz music. Include instead a flat seven note (b7 or dom7) and start feeling the blues (another indicator here will be your face starting to contort and twist to the side). We can play an instrument and add consonance or dissonance depending on our mood. We could use interesting or odd effects to our instrumentation to create something artistic. Hearing these things can immediately vaporize our current conception of reality, and it does so by really simple (physical process) yet inexplicable (emotional outcome) means.

Eventually, we can hear music when it is not there. While reading a book or looking at a painting (or maybe even eating), we can plug in the sounds to accompany the "picture" (or taste), and complete our experience. Like everything else artistic, there is an unyielding depth of emotion and creativity and technique to acquire. The trenches are so deep with music - because of the myriad variables involved - that it would take something inconceivably spectacular to render this particular art useless, or even boring. The fluidity and pliability of music allow for endless combinations of ideas. The biggest creative treasure trove would, in my opinion, lie right here with music.

I originally planned a chapter where I went on and on about music, its history, and my story of becoming a musician. I threw in talk of Vivaldi, Debussy, Ray Charles, Dylan, Hendrix, James Taylor, and Radiohead. I shortened it considerably. (I already have one really long chapter in this section, and I think that is probably enough.) As always, the thing to remember is staying engaged in the possibilities. If you do not play any instruments, you should try to pick one up and play. The new emotions you will discover will open you up to another world — a world where you are new to yourself, and the people around you seem to make a little more sense. If you do not consider playing, consider listening and studying every kind of music that you can greedily imbibe. Being imbued with a sense of understanding and patience is a natural result of becoming a better listener of music. Whether physically or emotionally (or both), you can learn to strike a "chord" of harmony, both with others and yourself.

Before I repeat too many of the same maxims, or ramble any worse that I have already done, let me end this chapter and follow with some final thoughts on how art can improve our lives.

Ch. 19 LIFE IN THE TRENCHES

"Mom…I'm a Liberal Arts major." This being a lamentable phrase that all parents dread - usually followed by said parents fainting in the floor. It isn't that they want their kids to be unhappy in some menial job pushing around pencils. Those jobs, however, are ones that guarantee a decent standard of financial living, and some degree of security. This is all that practical and caring parents want. Nevertheless I always hated the question, "What are you doing with your life?" or "What do you plan on doing?" Plan on doing? I beg your pardon, but all of life I believe to be a process of doing, no matter what I happen to be "doing." And am I the only humble one to admit that I will never quite "figure it out"? Indeed, I don't know that I even want to. Figuring it out sounds a bit too comfortable and, frankly, a life that is done doing. I do not ever want to be done doing.

The good thing about this philosophy of life is that it is not a dogmatic one. It is one that seamlessly weaves idealism through the threads of reality. I would also suggest, unlike many public motivators who appear too idealistic, that everyone have a safety career. The difference is that those menial jobs do not have to hinder our advances toward idealism and toward happiness. Not being able to run away and chase the rainbow over those sun-embroidered mountains is nothing to lose sleep over. We get to do these things in our minds any time we want. We may have to set our alarm and rise to sounds of city machines clamoring in a new day risen, but luckily this existence is not Orwell's "Nineteen Eighty-Four." We are not convicted of thought crime; we can lose ourselves as deep into our heads as we wish, with little recourse to the "real world" that surrounds us. Yes, we must do our jobs and yes we must have financial security, but this reality is only as constricting as we let it become. We need money, but we do not need that much of it. We need to live and eat to survive, but we do not need it to make us happy. We need to follow basic societal rules and mores, but we can still discover ourselves in that world of rules and mores. Happiness is not immutable – it, and the source of it, can change – and it is not contingent upon our complete physical and financial freedom. In fact, our *true* freedom is contraindicated by this perceived sense of freedom. If I had every chance to do what I wished, I would still wish for what I did not have. Yes, true freedom is found within the tumult and constraints of a regular life. As most of us are constrained by and quartered inside a regular life, where *else* would we discover ourselves? If it is the only place and opportunity, then we have to do what we have to do.

If we can accept reality – as I argued for in the first part of this book – losing ourselves in artistic pursuits can still fit the agenda. I may not be able to chase stars and museum-hop all over the world, but I can buy a telescope and an art book to keep me busy. Wanting to be everywhere and doing everything artistic is a side effect of this philosophy. Once in the trenches we want more and more. Theoretically this is a great thing, but in reality it can leave us longing and emotionally dejected. Recall the chapter on attachments. (I address this criticism more fully at the end of the book.) I cannot backpack across Europe, sip wine from the vineyards in France, or play bongos in a Puerto Rican town square. I cannot afford the time or costs to study sculptures and paintings in Italy, visit the wonder of the LHC (Large Hadron

Collider) in Bern, or craft lenses for famous photographers in China. I realistically cannot do many things that I want to do. However, one telling fact is that I *do* want it in the first place. I have the desire to eat life until I am no longer able to stuff my gullet. The insatiable hunger to engage in whatever is out there (while time's winged chariot hurries near) is what I hope to impart to you, Dear Reader.

It is up to us to accept a life that is in part composed of boring meetings, low pay, feelings of claustrophobia and seasickness, and cosmic "unfairness." But it is also up to us to go get what we can when we can get it. A life elevated by the arts and artistic pursuits is something attainable, and the first step is to simply understand that fact and walk through the gates. This type of life can slip through our hands if we are not careful to notice the faint, distant glimmer of those gates. It reminds me of Carl Sandburg's poem, "Fog." I replace 'fog' with 'life':

> The life comes
> on little cat feet
>
> It sits looking
> over harbor and city
> on silent haunches
> and then moves on

What does a life in the trenches mean for us? What can we reasonably hope to achieve? The word "achievement" sounds embroiled with the perennial idea of finished results. If this is the case then we may "achieve" very little. No, what this life means is the constant struggle and journey of discovering our potential, and discovering common ground with other people. Will you become a famous, globetrotting photographer? Will you even be capable of fairly calling your self a "photographer"? Perhaps. It does not matter. Allow your self to fall into the looking glass and discover what that can do for your life. That's it. The same applies to cooking and enjoying foods, painting, BJJ, or playing music. (I did not include many things that also interest me: gardening, sculpting, bird watching, dancing, filmmaking, acting, and so much more.) The depths are rewarding on their own merits, because the potential for personal growth is endless. The devil may be in the details, but I will have to take the risk. Actually, forget the devil, *life* is in the details.

A life out of the trenches means not finding your true potential for happiness and personal growth. It entails not truly understanding your fellow creatures and what they can offer your life. It means not fully caring about what makes others happy. It is entirely possible to be wrong or confused about being happy, or that we have secured a solid grasp on maximizing our happiness. We could think this and easily be spinning our wheels and simply turning in place. Some ways of living are "better" in the sense of maximizing happiness (not just pleasure or enjoyment), and those ways involve a process; sometimes this is an arduous process that involves stumbling and feelings of inadequacy. These feelings, though, ultimately drive us further than we ever imagined. What is the alternative? Stone-faced stoicism? Ask yourself that question. We may avoid feelings of pain and struggle by never entering through the gates, but a superficial life would be the result. We get out of life what we put into it; this includes, if we so choose, a life that is no real life at all. This would just be feigning life. Is that truly acceptable? We have to decide if we want no substantive feelings from life, or if we want to take it all in. A life in the trenches is one where we truly learn what it means to be in touch with not only ourselves, but also with others and what it means to enjoy a meaningful existence.

If you are on board thus far, we now have one main section left to uncover. The following section does two things. It covers the importance and necessity of science in our lives, and it also covers the basic skeleton of how we seem to live our lives. Our lives are often simpler than considerations of artistic endeavors and their philosophical underpinnings. I take some time to give some thought to practical considerations in a life that requires pragmatism (lest we float away completely on a cloud of idealism). A new car, an open road, and now we turn to the spare tire, fresh oil, and mileage concerns.

How do you feel so far? A little overwhelmed, yet? Good. That means you already have one foot in the trenches and are testing out the waters. You might already be fully submerged. Either way, I'll see you on the other side.

SCIENCE AND OUR LIVES

Isn't it sad to go to your grave without ever wondering
why you were born? Who, with such a thought, would
not spring from bed, eager to resume discovering
the world and rejoicing to be a part of it?
– Richard Dawkins

INTRODUCTION

We have come a long way so far and we are closing in on the
finish line. Part three of this book consists of several smaller points
concerning science and our lives. I've written this section of the
book as one chapter with a few different subheadings, as I felt
that was the best way to approach the content. It will be a lengthy
chapter (and a short overall section), but it will be partitioned into
easily discernable and readable sections.

I also start this section of the book discussing various aspects
of science, and how and why it is important to our lives. I talk
about why understanding our relationship to it can lead to a more
engaged and exciting life, as well as one that is grounded and
amenable to a stable conception of reality. The second "part" of
this chapter I talk about our lives in their day-to-day circumstances
and situations. I could have made two different chapters for the
first and second mini-topics, butIeventually opted for one long
chapter with a few related ideas, under different subheadings. This
discussion of "our lives" leads nicely out of the last main section
of the book and into the last chapter (preceding the conclusion)
where I address possible criticisms of my thesis. Much of that
chapter will detail the ideas tossed around at the end of this one.
The ultimate reason for including part three of the book was to
point out how living a normal life like a regular person does not
immediately vitiate artistic/philosophical potential. We all want

to stay grounded, live basically and frugally - both financially and emotionally - and just get on being happy without too much difficulty. I can see and agree with this; that is why it is important to talk about why everything in this book is still useful and amenable with "everyday" life. This part, then, in our analogy about road trips, is taking into view practical and safety concerns for our trip. For although we may have a new working car and an itinerary set out for us, part of us all is still afraid to be too adventurous and worries about mechanical malfunction, lack of gas money, and whether or not our destination will be better than the place we came from.

Part three can feel a bit disjointed, but it is important information for becoming a student of life... and learning to feel comfortable with it.

CH. 20 SCIENCE AND OUR LIVES

After sleeping through a hundred million centuries we have
finally opened our eyes on a sumptuous planet, sparkling
with color, bountiful with life. Within decades we must
close our eyes again. Isn't it a noble, an enlightened way of
spending our brief time in the sun, to work at understanding
the universe and how we have come to wake up in it? This
is how I answer when I am asked—as I am surprisingly
often—why I bother to get up in the mornings.
– Richard Dawkins

Science

Science is typically seen as (when it is actually thought about)
a necessary but invasive aspect of our lives. Some people do
not consider it necessary – some think it even pernicious or
corrupting - but I do not pay them any service in this book; I do
not have the patience and energy to deal with science *deniers* (like
Creationists or "faith-healers," and other similarly dangerous
people). No, this chapter - and the book - is for the individuals
who care enough to parse and sift through information. It is
for people who want to learn more from life, people who care
about gaining new knowledge, and people who will hear new
arguments.

The above-mentioned folks – the ones to whom I devote this book – are often just misled or confused about what can make them happy. Science is not seen as something emotionally or artistically helpful. Science is just seen as progress of a sort that more or less gets us through our lives. Some people will go so far as to cast aspersions on the scientific enterprise because it kills the beauty of art and philosophy. At any rate they do not see how helpful science is. They ignore that they could not finish a single day without the fruits of science's labor. Examples would include: transportation to and from work, electricity, clean water and food, medical treatment or medication, and the ATM that spits out our payday cash (that one is important). In short, people are so embroiled in the effects of science that they forget it even exists. It's like coming alive in a dollhouse and thinking you are actually real, or maybe living in a matrix reality while convincing yourself that your fabricated world is real. In other words, if you are surrounded by it you just become a part of it. It is important we do not forget what gets us through the day.

Science, however, is so much more brilliant than the ingenious daily assistant. Science, much like art, can lead us to gorgeous vistas of new opportunity for our lives. And America could use a few more kids who explore the wonders of the body, of the sky, and of things unseen. Another gratifying thing is that, much like philosophy, anybody can be a scientist. You do not need a lab coat and goggles and a fat brain to be a scientist. A sense of wonder is all that is necessary. That is in large part been the *sine qua non* of this book – just cast out that net and become more engaged. That is all that is necessary to start.

Let us take a look at some of the scientific things that matter to us. I paint a few little vignettes, and will let you research further on your own. As there is no need for me to say what others have said better, and to whom I am so indebted for their work, I will heavily quote other work throughout this chapter.

The Magisterial Brain

The brain is fascinating in that it is amazingly complicated in its ability to do stuff – like make us think there is an "us" in there somewhere. It is about as queer as the universe itself in that respect. JBS Haldane, a very important biologist back in the day (and, even though dead, now), once said something very telling: "Now, my own suspicion is that the universe is not only queerer than we suppose, but queerer than we *can* suppose." There is a beautiful sentiment from another evolutionary biologist (alive today), Jerry Coyne. He says this of our brains: "But there is something even more wondrous. We are the one creature to whom natural selection has bequeathed a brain complex enough to comprehend the laws that govern the universe. And we should be proud that we are the only species that has figured out how it came to be." It all starts there. Just imagine what our brains do for us. Our brains have created an entire world for us. There is so much good reading on these topics. I have had to really dial back what I wished to share in this book.

I will provide a very apt and lengthy quote from philosopher, Thomas Metzinger – a professor who is experimentally active in the neurosciences. This passage can be found in his book, *The Ego Tunnel*.

> The conscious brain is a biological machine – a reality
> engine – that purports to tell us what exists and what
> doesn't. It is unsettling to discover that there are no
> colors out there in front of your eyes. The apricot-pink

of the setting sun is not a property of the evening sky; it is the property of the internal *model* of the evening sky, a model created by your brain. The evening sky is colorless. The world is not inhabited by colored objects at all. It is just as your physics teacher in high school told you: Out there, in front of your eyes, there is just an ocean of electromagnetic radiation, a wild and raging mixture of different wavelengths. Most of them are invisible to you and can never become part of your conscious reality. What is really happening is that the visual system in your brain is drilling a tunnel through this inconceivably rich physical environment and in the process is painting the tunnel walls in various shades of color. *Phenomenal* color. *Appearance.* For your conscious eyes only.

That is a neat passage depicting how cool and interesting our brains are. I suggest also reading David Eagleman's book, *Incognito*, for an easy breakdown on the brain and how it works for us. Our brains usually have us believe that there is a controller at the wheels, but that isn't the case.

Metzinger again: "Nevertheless, as I have emphasized, there is no little man inside the head. In addition, weaker versions don't take the phenomenology really serious. But there is no one doing the waking up, no one behind the scenes pushing the Reboot button, no transcendental technician of subjectivity." I am not delving into a discussion of determinism and compatibilism – two schools of thought concerning free will – but, suffice it to say for now, no one disagrees that the deep recesses of the brain are hard at work just throwing thoughts and ideas into our consciousness. What else could happen? How could you think a thought before you actually think it? Where did it come from? If I ask you to think a famous movie star and you choose Robert Redford, can you account for why you did not choose, say, Angelina Jolie? The thought simply occurred to you, as if it was thrown up from the well below. For two somewhat competing schools of thought on the subject – and two readable and interesting accounts of the matter – I suggest Sam Harris' *Free Will* and Michael Gazzaniga's *Who's In Charge?*

These discussions are akin to the "ultimate meaning" ones mentioned earlier in the book. I asked how rocks and gas could have meaning for us. In some sense, the matter of the brain and free will falls into the same category. Understanding how the brain works – or at least the amazing attributes the brain possesses – can help us get through life with, if nothing else, at least a small dose of reality. When reality colors our existence, we can make better choices about our lives. The conversation can at least lead to more informed decisions and thought processes.

When we talk about our brains in this matter, we are not talking about fatalism. We still have a sense of "we," and this does matter. We can still change our lives, even if the deep recesses of our minds are hidden to us. According to a causal view of things that happen, if someone gives us pep talks then that, in turn, affects the deep pits of our brains and what it will next produce. So, there is a mechanical sort of determinism happening, but our conception of living existentially (see chapter three) is still very much safe. How cool is it, though, to understand the crazy nature of our brains and physical systems? Being engaged in this way is another important way to be engaged in life, because the brain is ultimately causing us to live those lives.

The Brain and Morality

Another area that should be of concern to us is how our brains interact with the world to inform a strong idea of ethics. Once more I let others make the compelling case. Namely, I use the well-known Pat Churchland for this goal. She is a professor of philosophy, notably a neurophilosohpher who works with neuroscientists (which is what most philosophers of mind are doing these days...metaphysics, in many respects, has fallen from favor and does not play quite the role it once did). These passages are taken from her book, *Braintrust*.

> What gets us around the world is mainly *not* logical deduction (derivation). By and large, our problem-solving operations – the figuring out the reasoning – look like a *constraint satisfaction process*, not like a deduction or the execution of an algorithm.

And again:

> More simply, mammals are motivated to learn social practices because the negative reward system, regulating pain, fear, and anxiety, responds to exclusion and disapproval, and the positive reward system responds to approval and affection.

Often times, there is no "right" answer to these problems.

> Often there are better or worse choices, but no uniquely right choice; in such cases constraint satisfaction does its business – balancing and harmonizing and settling on a suitable decision.

She goes on to discuss a wide array of biological and philosophical things, but goes on to say something very important.

> His point is that the process of reflecting on alternatives, understanding history and human needs, seeing things from the perspective of others, and talking it through with others can lead us to better evaluations of a social practice in the long run. Better, that is, than relying on self-appointed moral authorities and their list of rules.

She mentions many interesting things about the brain as well. I do not have time to really go into all of the wonderful things I have highlighted and earmarked in this book. The last thing I will quote from her book is one of the main points I wish to impart.

> None of this discussion implies that science can solve all moral dilemmas, nor that even scientists or philosophers are morally wiser than farmers or carpenters. But it does suggest that we should be open to the possibility that a deeper understanding of the nature of our sociality may shed on certain of our practices and institutions, and cause us to think more wisely about them.

This is important for us in more ways than one. For the specific purposes of this book, these are good examples of why it is important to be engaged in life. It is impossible to be fully engaged on what it means to live a life while ignoring science. Thinking about why we make decisions or why we think certain ways is important, because we may wish to inform or improve our lives with this very knowledge. By not delving into our physical systems and how they affect our daily lives, we may not ever fully understand who we are or what kind of life we are living. It is possible to live more happily by working to change our attitudes about these matters. Science, in fact, shows us that we could not have learned to be creative (including creating culture) or artistic without the physical aspects of our pasts. Science, it seems, can be the most beautiful discovery of all.

Bridging the Gap Between Art and Science

To use one last Pat Churchland quote to start: "The complaint that a scientific approach to understanding morality commits the sin of scientism does really exaggerate what science is up to, since the scientific enterprise does not aim to displace the arts or humanities. Shakespeare and Mozart and Caravaggio are not in competition with protein kinases and micro RNA." While art and science are not in competition, I feel impelled to point out that not only is science itself beautiful because of all the wonderful discoveries about the world, but we could easily have not been here at all or had the brain to do what we do. I quote extensively from Chip Walter's *Last Ape Standing*.

> We owe it to ourselves to unravel the riddles of our evolution because we, more than any other animal, *can*. If we don't, we stand no chance of comprehending who we really are as individuals or as a species. And only by understanding can we hope to solve the problems we create. To not understand how we came into the universe damns us to remain mystified by our mistakes, and unable to build a future that is that is not simply human, but also humane.

We see there Walter talking about becoming engaged in our shared past, and why it matters in living a life of understanding and compassion – a life which presumably would be happier (some of this was discussed in chapter eight). He goes on to point out that the arts wouldn't be arts without the evolution of the brain and culture.

> It's true other tools and technologies had been around millions of years, and they require creativity, but they are not examples of self-expression or symbolic thinking the way a piece of sculpture, a painting, language, or a song are. The timing of this matters because creative self-expression became possible when our brains reached a certain critical, but as yet undefined, level. Its emergence marks a watershed event in human evolution, arguably *the* watershed event.

We could get on without knowing that information (as many most likely do), but doesn't it give you a thrilling sense of understanding and concomitant humility to know this – that our artistic and cultural successes and abilities are tied to the evolution of our brains? It may not. For many, however, understanding this allows them to engage further in a life where there are plenty of meaningful things, things that you cannot buy and that are forever fulfilling and intriguing. If the question, "who are we?" matters, then engaging in life through the scientific enterprise has to be a priority. I'll allow Walter to once again make the case.

> When you look at us this way - a lifelong child with a mind itching to play, and famished for surprise

– you can see how the power for creating originality out of random experiences, could have taken us from a mere ten-thousand or so primates seventy-five thousand years ago, scrambling back from the abyss of extinction, to seven billion creatures who have not only populated every corner of the planet, but managed to rocket away from it a few times to orbit and land elsewhere in the solar system. By connecting the surprising experiences and ideas we spawn or stumbles across, and then sharing them with one another, we have been able to construct great edifices of new knowledge – Pythagoras's geometry, Newton's and Leibniz's calculus, the wheel, clocks and longbows, the Saturn V rocket and the silicon chip and balalaikas, silk paintings, the telescope, money, sailing ships and steam engines, kissing and language, music of all kinds and toys of every imaginable stripe, chess, baseball, sculpture, and Van Gogh's *Starry Night* – all of it out of the combined, interlocked, unique imaginings of millions of minds shaped by billions of surprises shared in trillions of exchanges to create the chaotic, astonishing, tumultuous stew we call human culture. In this sense, we are a race of continually startled, and startling, creatures.

Anyone else get goose bumps? I think that is enough said on that idea. I could not add anything to that without appearing parochial and underwhelming.

The quote at the beginning of this chapter by Richard Dawkins is one of the most beautiful sentiments – if not *the* most beautiful – I have ever read and contemplated. That sums up this chapter, this book, and my life. What could we want? How much beauty can you take? Because the world of science – the one that elucidates the real world around us – can display all of the beauty you can possibly handle. The beauty of explaining a rainbow is just as beautiful as poetry written about a rainbow. Science is not art, but art is usually written about what science explains. They are two sides of the same token. Poetry is written about the beauty of a rainbow, and science actually *explains* what makes it appear beautiful[10]. In one sense or another, we are writing about how we perceive the real world. Science explains that world. The scientific enterprise isn't just useful; it is as beautiful as art or philosophy because of its ability to constantly astound us and keep us busy in the trenches. It is also breathtaking because it is so humbling, as it puts us in our rightful places in the cosmos. Charles Darwin said, "There is grandeur in this view of life" when surveying the happenstance of nature. I agree. Nature can be so beautiful and simultaneously so ugly. But both the good and bad happening as it will is truly the most beautiful aspect of all. We would all do well to be engaged in the world around us. We live in that world, and those things are happening to us anyway. Why would we *not* do this? What's to gain from *that*? You now know very well what you could lose: the few decades you have in the sun, with nothing to show for it.

Our Lives

So, maybe we do not really care if we have anything to show for it. However, I think if we start to break down that statement we find that it is not really true that we don't care. What is true is to say is that it is difficult to conceive of doing things differently. We

---

[10] Richard Dawkins discusses this subject - and John Keats - beautifully in *Unweaving the Rainbow*.

establish patterns of operation and routines to stabilize our lives. If we did not establish these patterns our lives would be too hectic or erratic, and we would feel insecure about floating through a life unhinged. We *have* to have routines. This is certain. However, we should also realize that spontaneity is important in order to throw a wrench into a stultifying monotony. It is possible, as we are all too aware, to be bogged down in the morass of machine-like patterns of living. Okay. So, we can easily recognize that a balance needs to be met. Check.

The problem is not that people cannot see this duality. The problem is that people have a hard time achieving this balance in practice. It can be done, though, and is, in fact, done by many people. Being happy in our ability to be productive during the day, as well as occasionally being able to find time for a drive out in the country (or enjoy a picnic), is nice. The point of this book, however, has been to show much more than that can be available to us. The first dichotomy is not a false one. It is just one that leaves the world black and white; it is a dichotomy that does not recognize the trenches of life and the happiness that is culled from exploring them.

Many people claim they are happy. Of that bunch, some are deluding or lying to themselves, and some are indeed actually happy. If there were some happiness-measuring device, then the latter group would pass the test. I am not arguing that some people are not truly happy as they are. I am arguing that the qualities, pursuits and philosophy that this book espouses can *increase* that happiness. Maybe there is such a thing as too much happiness, but I'm inclined to doubt it. I've never heard anyone exclaim, "Arg! If only I wasn't so happy all the time! My extra interests in photography and filmmaking are ruining my life. And I hate being so patient, controlled, and humble all of the time. What a life! I would like to go back to my shitty nine-to-five. I was so much less happy – and therefore, happier – then!"

I half-jokingly use this *reductio ad absurdum* (reducing the argument to absurdity), but it makes sense. Just think about it. Is there a decent argument *against* my position? I believe I have thoroughly argued throughout the book that each of the bits of philosophy, and each artistic pursuit, hold their own merits. So if we can agree upon those particulars, then holding a position of just *employing* these things makes perfect sense. Yes, your life could be busier as a result. But it is a busyness that is fun as well as permanently rewarding. Your life may be more intense. This is also a good thing in the same way being busy is. Living in the trenches presents obstacles, but I feel I have shown that they are worth the time and energy. I will spend some more time in chapter twenty-one addressing criticisms or concerns with being a student of life.

Suffice it to say here, as I finish the last main section of the book, being a student of life has no viable alternative. We are not students of one particular discipline. We are not just filling the shoes and playing the role of: father, mother or athlete; musician, chef, or painter; or those who "belong" to a particular tribe, nation, or faith. These things, of course, help compose our lives. We figure out a livable routine, and we follow that routine; these are the lives we lead. Living a complete life stuffed with potential happiness, though, comes from being engaged in life *in general*. It is a peering into those lives that matters. We could change, add, or subtract, but the point is that we are always deeply involved.

Always be ready and willing to dig in and try or think a little harder or deeper. Ask the tough questions. Question yourself, and always wonder whether or not you are doing enough in the few decades of existence you have. If you are lucky, you may get to count those decades as your own. For my money, there seems to be no reason in not accepting one large, inclusive, and permanent role – that of a student of life.

In our analogy we addressed practical concerns. It turns out there was a spare tire and an endless supply of oil already waiting in our new car. Can we live as a student of life engaged and immersed in art, philosophy, and science? Of course we can. It is no problem at all. Our lives change, but they can change as much we want and at whatever pace we want. It is life changing, but yet it isn't. Maybe you thought you wouldn't see a statement like the last one on a hundred fifty or so pages into a book like this. I told you at the beginning that isn't the typical self-help book, and that philosophy can appear obtuse or strange. The point, Dear Reader, is that "our lives" are compatible with this new ideology. You have a new car, an open road, and every amenity that you once had for practical considerations. Not a bad life. And hey, not a regrettable idea to write this book, either. I'm kind of happy I was engaged enough to see it in front of me.

CH. 21 CRITICISMS

Before closing out I thought it might be useful to answer some possible criticisms or concerns about the themes in this book. Hopefully you have made it thus far in the book - this is obviously the case if you are reading this, unless you are just browsing around the contents of the book. There are a few things that I find myself saying in response to the content in my book. There are others who have, in one form or another, expressed certain misgivings about some of the things I have written. I only address here what I feel to be legitimate concerns or questions. The easiest and neatest way to do this is by formatting this chapter in FAQ style, where I assume the questions you may have and desire for me to answer. I cannot foresee all questions, and I apologize if I am presumptuous for including such a chapter in the first place. I simply care so much about this concept of engaging in life, art and philosophy that I have thought extensively about my content and how it will be received. In fact, I think more books should include such a section. I wish for all of you to close this book thoroughly convinced and ready to take seriously my suggestions. If I did not feel so strongly about it, I would not have bothered to write this book anyway. It is, of course, not possible - or perhaps even reasonable - that everyone should be convinced. There will be others who will have found the wording and concepts difficult. There will even be some who find the arguments and concepts too facile and tantamount to low-hanging fruit. Fair enough. Such is the case for putting out information in a book. Such is life, for that matter. At any rate I hope that I can at least touch on and clear up a few criticisms or questions in the course of this chapter.

Doesn't your realist philosophy conflict with your idealism in Part Two?

This initially appears that it would be the case. I made the case throughout the book that engaging in life, art, and philosophy would lead to a happier existence. If you keep that in the back of your mind the entire time, that specific conflict seems to dissolve. It is really only a conflict on paper or in some literary book. Indeed, my approach to life is a very balanced one. I taper my idealism in part two with heavy doses of realism in parts one and three. I do not do this for the sake of moderation. I do this because it makes sense to me that this should be the case. Some people are too idealistic and have their heads too far in the clouds. And some people do not have their heads above the ground, much less high enough to smell that sweet air above.

Another interesting thing is that my "realism" in the first and third parts is idealistic in some sense. It is a call to rise above or look beyond the boring "realities" of everyday life. In the same breath, however, it is very adamantly realistic – it shuns materialism, religiosity, and unthinking language mores. It also invites the sometimes-unwelcome realities of our mortal clocks, the need to understand one another better, and losing our sense of self in which we are so often involved. Considering our lives in the stark light of certain realities only helps to wipe clean the slate for more ideal pursuits. In this sense, idealism and realism are two very important sides to one invaluable coin.

Who are you to write this book? *–Or-* **How do you think you have "figured it out"?**

This complaint is akin to the old, "You're telling me how I should live? Ha!" I can imagine some indignant faces after reading leading phrases like, "If we can only do X, we will be happier." I answer this realizing that many who picked up the book were looking for something along these lines. Yet, still many will scoff at such broad brush stroking.

Let me clear the elephant from the room. *I am nobody.* I am perfectly fine with being a nobody. One can be a nobody and write these books. I am not claiming to be anyone special or important. That's part of the point. Really anyone can learn to step into life with full-throttle engagement. Thinking philosophically takes no training; it just takes a little practice. Even learning technical or academic philosophy can be done by anyone. I remember picking up my first history of philosophy book by Frederick Copleston. It was difficult but it took no "smarts" – in the mathematical, quick-on-the-feet sense. I'm terrible at that type of thinking and computing, and therefore make *no* claim on being smart. You do not have to have gone to college or have any degrees. I did, but I have little to show for it. In fact, I am starting to believe "higher education" does very little in the way of practical results. Millions of people never attend a college and make more money and have better jobs than those who did attend. This is important. Both of these groups, however, can be oblivious to the thesis of my book. The point I'm making is that anyone of any background can increase their happiness by fully immersing themselves in the moments of life – in both thinking *and* doing.

As for the second question, I have not figured out anymore than that I am constantly figuring *it* out. That really is the battle. The battle is to understand that we can never know enough about life and our places in it to achieve a stolid, unflinching certitude. I am like Socrates. He realized that he might be considered wise because he realized he really didn't know anything; indeed, the only way he obtained *any* knowledge is by admitting he really didn't possess much knowledge. In this sense, this book is following the Socratic footsteps all the way down the road and into the autumn sunset, out of view. Just realize that there is always something to figure out and always something to learn. My goal with the book is just to share that.

Elitism

One of the most illegitimate complaints I hear often is that suggesting to people what they might do to increase their happiness is considered "elitist." It is a dumb complaint but one that is sadly ubiquitous. It is so popular that I felt the need to address it.

The reason that people feel their feelings have been trampled upon is that they themselves did not realize the matter first. Let that sink in. Everyone always suggests to friends and others to think certain ways – about religion, politics, social concerns, and everything else. However, when someone suggests to *them* some way to view these things, that person then becomes a know-it-all elitist, trespassing on their subjective rights and feelings. Anyone can hear these arguments and choose to ignore them. What else can I do? This is no different than me (or you) arguing anything else. I am suggesting that people can be wrong about their happiness (as I pointed out with our hypothetical drug addict). Why is this a taboo matter? You can do one of two things: you can read and contemplate my points and decide I am wrong - in which case no harm no foul - or you can read my arguments and decide I make a decent point - in which case you reevaluate the way you go about things. I welcome a refutation or debate with my philosophical points. I would find it hard to rebut many of these points, but I would certainly hear out such attempts. The "art" section was just a list of options on what you may want to pursue and why it would help increase your happiness. If suggesting ideas for *increasing* happiness (as some people may be happy without any artistic pursuits) is an elitist attitude (it isn't), then I will have to assume the role of an elitist. If this is the case I gladly accept the appellation.

I'm too busy to become more "involved," as you say

This is a very fair, realistic, and legitimate complaint. While some arguments may be unwarranted, this one is probably the best. It is certainly true to say that busyness pervades a good portion of society. Our schedules give us purpose, but they also run us into the ground. Although this appears a fair criticism, it is entirely possible to follow the expressions in this book through to their fruition. Let us say my thesis was different. Let us say I wrote about how paragliding can make your life better. That is so specific that there would easily be problems with doing this. If this were the case many people would simply have to live unhappily. What if, instead of my proposal, I wrote of the necessity of travelling? In order to truly achieve happiness one must spend a considerable amount of time travelling the world. There are clearly time and money constraints with this lifestyle. Either you have the time and money for this or you do not. A majority of the global population does not have the luxury (both the time and money) to travel to this extent. Even if this were true – that travelling made people the happiest – those facts would remain the same.

Am I asking anything of the sort? The philosophy bit asks of nothing of the sort. In fact, it propounds the notion of ridding ourselves of materialistic concerns such as money, and it asks us to think harder about the concept of time and to simply slow down and look around. I mention also that you do not have to give up your money or give up your time – just that you consider tapering these things. Remember, I live in the real world also. I also suggest that you learn to control your reaction to not being able to do the things that you may want, such as travelling.

Pursuing artistic endeavors may or may not cost money. If we are the ones *creating* art it may cost us some money. It will cost money to buy a camera or perhaps some local food for cooking. It will cost money to buy an instrument or paint and canvas. Maybe even just one of these pursuits would be difficult to afford, but it can be done. This is not a book about controlling our budgets, but I find that most could give up booze or smokes on the weekend, get one less item for the car, buy cheaper gas, or maybe eat cheap, homemade food for a while. There are many ways to increase even a small budget. The same idea goes for increasing our time for these pursuits or activities. If we evaluate it we find our amount of time can be increased - if not substantially then just enough to make it count.

All I am asking in this book is that you become more *aware* and engaged with the life around you. Question others and question yourself. Appreciate details and nuance in ideas, arguments, and positions. Appreciate the arts in that they can help you learn more about others and your self. I think you will find your interest in *wanting* these things – and finding time to do them – will increase and become readily apparent. Eventually, the busiest of schedules can bend a little for our discerning minds. It becomes second nature to be philosophically involved in a worthwhile life. Pursuing and appreciating an art takes a little more time, but it can be achieved. Like usual, becoming myopic in these matters – *on either side of the aisle* – is a bad thing. But moderation is something about which I need not opine…you folks got that down.

What about bigger, more important philosophies of life? There are bigger fish to fry.

There might be a group of readers who will claim that my arguments are too facile and do not add anything to a philosophically burly notion of life. I would disagree with those people. In my view, although there is no groundbreaking academic philosophy (there was never meant to be), my arguments are not facile or even well known or appreciated. I think the ideas are easy to grasp, but I simply believe they are overlooked by a majority of people who are so busy living in the machine that they forget – or never knew – what made them truly tick. I expect some of the reaction to be surprise at newly heard ideas, and I also expect some of the reaction to be something like, "Oh yeah! I forgot that I used to feel this way." In the light of most "self-empowerment" books, and the dubious gurus who write them, this book I believe to be a necessary alternative.

And yet another group will argue that I did not cover what would seem yet even *more* facile and obvious points. They will say, "This seems like sideline philosophy. What about love and giving to charity? Those are surely more important." I will have to respectfully rejoin here: "DUH!" I asked myself daily throughout the writing of this book if there was a need for it to be written. Thankfully, I answered yes every day. I like to reduce arguments to absurdity before I attempt to make them. I do this to be sure that I have an argument worth making without looking silly. If the argument fails that test, then I do not employ it. I cannot imagine someone denying the power of love and selflessness as the most important tools for a happy life. What would that look like? "The world should run on cold hatred and solipsism. Arg, darn that love and giving!" That's obviously absurd. So, then, there was no need to write a book about the matter or even to include it. What has been said about those things to this extent is sufficient. I have nothing to add on the matter. *Of course* love and giving to people make the world a better place, and of course those things fulfill our lives. My arguments were geared toward adding happiness and fulfillment *on top* of the love and selflessness backbone. I'm not obviating the need for one or the other; I am simply combining them. Is too much happiness a bad thing? We have a hard enough time at it as it is. There is always room in our lives for more loving and more giving. Being a student of life may indeed put us in touch with a little more of both of those things. That is not something that should be overlooked. With that in mind, let's wrap this thing up shall we?

CONCLUSION

> The offer of certainty, the offer of complete security,
> the offer of an impermeable faith that can't give
> way, is an offer of something not worth having. I
> want to live my life taking the risk all the time that I
> don't know anything like enough yet; that I haven't
> understood enough; that I can't know enough;
> that I'm always hungrily operating on the margins
> of a potentially great harvest of future knowledge
> and wisdom. I wouldn't have it any other way.
> – Christopher Hitchens

In the popular comedy/action/drama flick, *City Slickers,* there is a memorable scene where Billy Crystal's character, Mitch, is meandering along in the great wide open on his horse, beside him Jack Palance's burly old, rough and tumble cowboy character, Curly. As they mosey along, in a beautiful summer afternoon amidst a classically Western backdrop, they begin to muse about their different lifestyles and what life means to them. Suddenly, Curly looks at Mitch and the following interaction occurs:

Curly: *Do you know what the secret to life is?*
Mitch: (light, pensive music plays) *No, what?*
Curly: *This* (holds up pointer finger)
Mitch: *Your finger?*

Curly: *One thing. Just one thing. You stick to
that and everything else don't mean shit.*
Mitch: *That's great, but...what's the one thing?*
Curly: *That's what you gotta figure out.*
Mitch: (left looking confusedly at his own
pointer finger sticking in his face)

That scene is still etched in my mind as one of the most intensely breathtaking moments in philosophical film. It's altogether beautiful and confusing and frustrating and uplifting and exasperating. In other words, it's good philosophy. What did Curly mean by the "one thing"? We have to figure that out for ourselves. The one thing we usually figure out is that there really is no "one thing" that will fully define us in any permanent sense. It is true to say, however, that it has to be our own self that figures it out. So, that quote is frustrating until you later realize what is meant by it. People want there to be some quick fix version of life, philosophy in a box. It took Mitch until the end of the film to realize the "one thing" is whatever he wants it to be. That one thing may change, but it will always be his. There is no "meaning of life." What a dumb idea. The real meaning of life is to give life a meaning – and only you can do that in your own way. One must engage in life, and a philosophy of life, to find and understand this. What's your one thing? Now is your time to think about it.

Something else to consider is the uncertain nature of life on top of constant push and pull decisions and struggles. Musicians speak of this all the time. They write about the indecision of a life loving the road, and hating never having a home life. These musicians are learned philosophers in this respect. (Renaissance philosopher, Michel de Montaigne, famously noted that fame and tranquility could never be bedfellows.) I spoke earlier of Joni

Mitchell. The Black Crowes sing of being "tired, but wiser for the time." John Mayer always rhapsodizes in longing melody about constantly struggling over the domestic home cat with a loving and reliable family, and the urge to unendingly take on the world. He says, "This house is safe and warm, but I was made to chase the storm; taking this whole world on with big ol' empty arms." In another song he says something very telling of many people's lives. "Life ain't short, but it sure is small; you get forever, but nobody at all – it don't come often and it don't stay long."

A real struggle for a lot of people is living as the peripatetic poet, and learning all you can and changing the world as you go. Pair that with the urge to settle and stay in a pair (or several pairs) of arms that loves you. The struggle is indicative of something bigger: *wanting it all out of life.* We want what we do not have. We always will. Why wouldn't we? Is it not natural to long for *every* experience there possibly is before our short run in the sun is done? I think so…and if not it should be. Not being able to conquer this hill results in existential angst about the decisions we make. But this is what it means to live a life engaged in that beautiful struggle. As Socrates would tell you, if you think you have it figured out you either did your calculations wrong, or do not understand what life is. I wrote this book for either one of those groups. Camus would tell us to face this struggle, and Sartre would tell us to recognize others in ourselves and to make the lives of those others more enjoyable.

Another example of this Manichean type of struggle is displayed in the film, *Up in the Air* (a romantic, philosophical drama). George Clooney's character, Ryan Bingham, is a bit of a professional heartbreaker – in more ways than one (shut the front door - George Clooney, you don't say!) His job requires his being on the road (or, technically, in the air) for most days in the year. He has no intention of settling down with a family and stable location. He is a free spirit. Throughout the film we see forces start to shape his thoughts, and he might then fall in love with a woman he meets along the way. If the film followed course, we would find Bingham playfully realizing the error of his ways and changing his mindset. Instead, the film takes a different course and he doesn't get his love after all. (Sorry for the spoiler.) In the "end," he is left in a more uncertain and confused state than where he, and the audience, started. There was no real resolution. There was no absolution either. That is how I like films to end from time to time, as that charts real life. Before the closing credits we see a beautiful sky at dusk, with remnants of dying sun bestriding the clouds (from the vantage point of flying in them). We hear Bingham's voice, and he says these last words: "Tonight, most people will be welcomed home by jumping dogs and squealing kids. Their spouses will ask about their day, and tonight they'll sleep. The stars will wheel forth from their daytime hiding places; and one of those lights, slightly brighter than the rest, will be my wingtip passing over." There is no way to know if Bingham has given up on the other type of life, but he is clearly comfortable where he thinks he belongs – up in the air. Life is uncertain and things are always "up in the air." As chapter two mentioned, being in control and accepting this type of uncertainty and vacillation will bring you into reality. This is the first step in attaining happiness, as it is the first inquiry into an engaged life.

The philosophy in my book is centered on becoming engaged in a realistic conception of life. We need to stay in control in a life where everything *clearly* does *not* happen for a reason. To accomplish this, we have to pay attention to our language, what others and we say, and what that actually means. We have to consider notions of time, immortality, and information overload if we are to become engaged in life. If we become aware that we are not special, and that our time should be spent considering other people, then we start to lead a happier life. We would do well also to enjoy the Mother Nature and what she has to offer, as well as what she can tell us about living a simple but involved life.

The philosophy is loosely integrated, but these are things I notice have been instrumental in changing people's lives. There is such a massive online community of people who have settled into similar philosophies or practice these philosophical tenets. I've heard personal testimony of lives changing for the better. Anecdotal evidence is far from "evidence," and I expect none of my readers to accept that as satisfactory. My Dear Readers, you could accept one or some of these principles, or perhaps even none of them. I can only humbly put them before you. They are large generalities, and in some ways are not really specific points about what to think or do.

The arts, of course, are specific suggestions. Again, picking something artistic to pursue is something that is completely subjective. Everyone will be interested and passionate about different things (and that fact is contingent upon many other factors). The main idea here, though, is to point out how the pursuit of these activities and modes of engaging allow for a much more deeply involved life, a life in the trenches where you and others always have goals to achieve and knowledge to acquire. Just *trying* to be involved or interested in something you are currently not is a huge first step in the right direction. That is what I argued in this book. The concepts I bring to the table may appear to some to be too obvious, or maybe too vague. I addressed this in the last chapter. It might appear to be this way, but I continue to notice so many people foundering in their own boredom or their own self-deception about their lives. It is obvious to me to approach life in this full-throttle manner, but to many individuals these particular ideas are not forthcoming. I felt the book needed to be written for these reasons – to possibly clear up what some folks might not be able to clear up for themselves. At any rate it can't be more shallow or jejune than the apparent majority of self-empowerment books. I'm not really empowering you; I am letting you see for yourselves how to do this. Or, at least I'm showing you how *you* can figure this out on your own. It is a starting point - or some scaffolding. It is not as if there are no problems with my life, and that I have it all figured out and under control at all times. But, again, this is not a warranted criticism of the book and its contents, as I have previously admitted this to be the case. The book is really a journey for everyone, including myself (damn it, I will not quote Frost!) I naturally admit fault or ignorance wherever necessary. I allow for debates and differences of opinion, and I can conceive of being in the wrong. However, I am prepared to fully defend any position I posited thus far. I've not "made it." But I have a figured out the way to begin that process and stay strong along the way. If I make several million dollars and discover that is really the true key, I will simply rescind my thoughts and pull the book from the shelves.

The last bit was on science and our lives. I took the time to defend the name and enterprise of science, as it is often maligned or simply just ignored. This is such a shame to witness, because our entire lives to some degree are centered on the scientific enterprise and the institutions established by that enterprise. Thinking about who we are as creatures has really allowed us to stand in awe of what we have become. As Chip Walter states in the previously quoted book, "The Last Ape Standing:"

> We are not only an animal that can explore a life not
> yet lived, and dream of a future we desire, we can also
> take hold of those dreams and make them come true.
> Out of a chaotic flux of random events in nature that

have no agenda and are utterly incapable of making any plans, we have evolved into a planning, agenda-making, dream conjuring creature. We are the first survival machines to also become living, breathing, imagination machines.

This is why reality is just as sensational and awe-inspiring as anything out of a fairytale. As Dawkins puts it, "The magic of reality is wonderful. Wonderful, and real. Wonderful *because* real." When I talk about our lives, I mean to do so in the sense that we usually live them; that is, a generally relaxed, stable life, free of general worries and injuries. I talked about this in the book, because it is thought that perhaps additional philosophies or activities will only complicate a life that is "hard enough as it is." This is a false assumption. Life may be more involved, but it is not more difficult in an absolute sense. Indeed, sometimes being in control and reflecting on matters that are important, alleviate the unnecessary complications in our lives. In this sense, the philosophy I promulgated would allay many of our concerns about a "complicated" existence. To some extent, learning to get on *without* the day-to-day hustle - as opposed to *adding* to it - is an important remedy to life on the move.

The artistic side of life should be pursued and that can become tiresome, but there is no fast rule about what and when and where. You can become passionate and involved in music, dancing, acting, and sculpting. You could do any number of things that would benefit your life. You, and nobody else, will have to decide what, if anything, is too much. The line can be drawn, and it is you who must draw it. One criticism I did not address in the last chapter is the one that insists the idea of pursuing artistic things can be overwhelming, and that it is impossible to be "good at" many things. This is probably true for most people. But the idea that we have to explore the infinite depths of every possible thing of artistic interest is one that is missing the point. It is a silly idea. The main point is that *recognizing* or *wanting* these things shows that you are on the right path to a life in the trenches. If you *want* to explore everything there is to explore, and *recognize* that there is no way your short life can supply the time and means to do so, you are probably on the right track. Finding a niche (or two, or three) is not hard to do once your brain starts to dig in and ask some questions.

Expressing nuance and subtlety, along with being as fair as possible, is the sign of a true progressive. There is always something to explore. What is waiting for you in a life of doing otherwise? It would seem to me to be one denuded of any real meaning. Reading this at sixteen and at sixty will allow for different perceptions of this idea. Besides the quote at the beginning of this conclusion, Christopher Hitchens is well known for another lovely sentiment that sums up my thoughts on this matter (and the book). "Take the risk of thinking for yourself, much more happiness, truth, beauty, and wisdom will come to you that way." Think for your self, but think hard and think deep. Always ask your self, "What does this mean?" and "am I being a student of life, or just floating through it?" Therein I think you will find some of the answers you need. Grab a friend, hold up your finger to them and ask them if they know the secret of life. Take that finger now and point to my section of the bookstore, if you don't mind.

What's left for me to say? I want to very briefly mention again why I bothered writing this book. It is the same reason you should become engaged in not only your self, but also in others around you. It is the reason that being a student of life leads to a happier existence. In the movie *Cloud Atlas* (mentioned earlier in the book), one of the characters was told his endeavor to help others would fail, and that he amounted to nothing more than a drop in the ocean. The character responded with this heart-wrenching gem: "But what is an ocean but a multitude of drops?"

All I could do was write this. And now I move on. The rest, friends, is up to you. My part is finished. Good luck to you, and greetings in the future.

In the words of kingpin blues legend, B.B. King, "If that ain't it, I quit."

ACKNOWLEDGEMENT

I feel compelled to say I struggled through one or more of the following to complete this project: privation and proper lack of financial support, the stinging desert sands of the arid Middle East (which would have been at least, as T.E. Lawrence says of it in the famous film, "clean") – as a journalist, naturally – or dutifully in front of an open bottle of Johnnie Walker Black. The last of the three conditions contains perhaps a nugget or two of truth. As it stands, my resume – as is often the case with first time writers – is uninspiringly meager. I hope to continue to write and find myself entrenched in the life and circumstances of a writer. Until then, I have but a paltry and rather un-writer-like dedication – and no whimsical postscript as of yet. Although my future list of comrades and acquaintances and "insiders" has yet to materialize, there are a few people I wish now to thank. The quaint and wonderful lady, Mrs. V.J. Hampton, had gone to extra trouble helping me gather my thoughts and guiding me through the self-publishing process. Her patience and experience – as well as her own very inspirational and unique photojournalistic poetry – has been more helpful than she probably knows. I want to thank my mother and father, as well as my wife, for continued financial support, allowing me to pursue happiness in this vein where they might put theirs temporarily on the backburner. My kids keep me sane and put a smile on my face. It's my hope that they will become avid students of life. Lastly, I issue a nod to Christopher Hitchens, one of the bravest men and public intellectuals of our or any time. Much of my intellectual inspiration came – and still comes – from him. I was lucky to have known his body of work (which, I suppose, leads me to indirectly thank social media and technology).

BIBLIOGRAPHY

Introduction

Elliot, T.S. Excerpt from *Little Gidding*. In *Songs For The Open Road* edited by The American Poetry & Literary Project, 47. New York: Dover Publication, Inc., 1999.

Thoreau, Henry David. Excerpt from *Walden*. In *The Portable Thoreau* edited by Carl Bode. New York: Penguin Group, 1947.

Ch. 1

For Albert Camus's philosophy: Internet Encyclopedia of Philosophy. http://www.iep.utm.edu/camus/#SH5c

Ch. 2

Whitman, Walt. Excerpt from *Song of the Open Road*. In *Songs For The Open Road* Edited by The American Poetry & Literary Project, 1. New York: Dover Publication, Inc., 1999.

Joni Mitchell Library. http://jonimitchell.com/library/view.cfm?id=1459.

Ch. 3

Harrison, Guy P. *50 Popular Beliefs That People Think Are True*. New York: Prometheus Books, 2012.

Sartre, Jean-Paul. *Existentialism and Humanism*. Connecticut: Yale University Press, 1946.

Incubus. *Make Yourself.* Sony Music Entertainment, 1999.

Ch. 4

Orwell, George. *Politics and the English Language*. http://orwell.ru/library/essays/politics/english/e_polit.

Rorty, Richard. *Philosophy And Social Hope*. England: Penguin Books, 1999.

Huxley, Thomas Henry. On the Reception of the Origin of Species in *The Life and Letters of Charles Darwin*. http://aleph0.clarku.edu/huxley/Book/Recep.html

Ch. 5

Internet World Stats. http://www.internetworldstats.com/stats.htm.

Global Mobile Statistics 2013. http://mobithinking.com/mobile-marketing-tools/latest-mobile-stats/a#smartphonepenetration.

Pew Internet. http://www.pewinternet.org/Commentary/2012/February/Pew-Internet-Mobile.aspx.

Ch. 6

Marvell, Andrew. Excerpt from *To His Coy Mistress*. In *A Treasury of Great Poems* compiled and selected by Louis Untermeyer, 484. New York: Galahad Books, 1993.

Caveman: A Interview with Michel Siffre. http://www.cabinetmagazine.org/issues/30/foer.php.

Jewsih Tv Network. *Is There an Afterlife?* – Christopher Hitchens, Sam Harris, David Wolpe, Bradley Artson Shavit. http://www.youtube.com /watch?v=UjKJ92b9Y04.

Ch. 7

Shelley, Percy Bysshe. Excerpt from *Ozymandias*. In *Immortal Poems of the English Language* edited by Oscar Williams, 295. New York: Pocket Books, 1952.

Webster, John. Excerpt from *All the Flowers of the Spring*. In *Immortal Poems*, 96.

Berring, Jesse. *The Belief Instinct*. New York: W.W. Norton & Company, 2011.

Cave, Stephen. *Immortality*. New York: Crown Publishing Group, 2012.

Dawkins, Richard. *The Selfish Gene*. New York: Oxford University Press, 1989.

Christoper Hitchens in debate with Jay Richards, January 2008. http://www.youtube.com/watch?v=HO129-RfhVE.

Sagan, Carl. *Pale Blue Dot*. New York: Random House, 1994.

Ch. 8

Joel, Billy. *We Didn't Start the Fire*. Columbia Records, 1989.

McCullough, David. "Why History." *Readers Digest*, December, 2002.

Cloud Atlas, DVD. Directed by Lana Wachowski, Tom Tykwer, and Andy Wachowski. Warner Bros., 2012.

Ch. 9

Blake, William. *Eternity*. In *Great Poems*, 607.

Herrick, Robert. Excerpt from *To the Virgins, to Make Much of Time*. In *Immortal Poems*, 97.

Ch. 10

Thoreau, Henry David. *I Was Born Upon Thy Bank River*. In *Great Short Poems* edited by Paul Negri. New York: Dover Publications, Inc., 2000.

Blake, William. *Great Things are Done when Men and Mountains Meet*. In *Songs for the Open Road*, 9.

Emerson, Ralph Waldo. Excerpt from *Nature*. In *The Essential Writings of Ralph Waldo Emerson* edited by Brooks Atkinson. New York: Random House, 2000.

Ch. 11

Millay, Edna St. Vincent. Excerpt from *Travel*. In *Songs for the Open Road*, 35.

Ch. 14

Steichen, Edward. Brainy Quote. http://www.brainyquote.com/quotes/authors/e/edward_steichen.html.

Dawkins, Richard. *The Blind Watchmaker*. New York: W.W. Norton & Company, 1996.

Ch. 15

Wilde, Oscar. Fine Dining Lovers. http://www.finedininglovers.com/stories/food-quotes-oscar-wilde/.

Bourdain, Anthony. *Medium Raw*. New York: Ecco, 2011.

Joel, Billy. *Scenes From an Italian Restaurant*, CD. From *The Stranger*. Columbia Records, 1977.

Welles, Orson. Good Reads. https://www.goodreads.com/author/quotes/67899.Orson_Welles.

Child, Julia. Good Reads. http://www.goodreads.com/
quotes/133360-in-france-cooking-is-a-serious-art-form-and-a.
Quek, Justin. Chattering Kitchen. http://chatteringkitchen.com/
culinary-quotes/.

Ch. 16

Putarch at BrainyQuote. http://www.brainyquote.com/quotes/
quotes/p/plutarch117780.html.

Picasso, Pablo. Thinkexist.com. http://thinkexist.com/quotation/
painting _is_just_another_way_of_keeping_a_diary/
217877.html.

Ch. 17

Gracie, Helio. Gracie Academy online. http://odysseywebs.org/
rosskeeping/.

Ch. 18

Nietzsche, Friedrich. Good Reads online. http://www.goodreads.
com/quotes /4590-without-music-life-would-be-a-mistake.
Huxley, Aldous. Good Reads online. http://www.goodreads.
com /quotes/4394-after-silence-that-which-comes-nearest-to-
expressing-the-inexpressible.

Ch. 20

Dawkins, Richard. Good Reads online. http://www.goodreads.
com/quotes/91783-after-sleeping-through-a-hundred-million-
centuries-we-have.

Haldane, JBS. Good Reads online. https://www.goodreads.com/author/quotes/63158.J_B_S_Haldane.

Coyne, Jerry. *Why Evolution Is True*. New York: Penguin Group, 2009.

Metzinger, Thomas. *The Ego Tunnel*. New York: Basic Book, 2009.

Chruchland, Pat. *Braintrust*. New Jersey: Princeton University Press, 2011.

Walter, Chip. *The Last Ape Standing*. New York: Walker Publishing, Inc, 2013.

Darwin, Charles. *On the Origin of Species*. New York: Barnes & Noble Books, 2004.

Conclusion

Hitchens, Christopher. Excerpt taken from a debate. Accessed on Bluejay's Way on Wordpress. http://bluejaysway.wordpress.com/2010/11/29/christopher-hitchens-incandescent/.

City Slickers, DVD. Directed by Ron Underwood. Castle Rock Entertainment, 1991.

Michel de Montaigne. Quote taken from *The Philosophy Book*. New York: DK Publishing, 2011.

Black Crowes. *Wiser Time*, CD. From *Amorica*. American Recordings, 1994.

Mayer, John. *Paradise Valley*, CD. Columbia Records and Sony Music, 2013.

Up in the Air, DVD. Directed by Jason Reitman. Paramount Pictures, 2009.

Dawkins, Richard. *The Magic of Reality*. New York: Free Press, 2011.

King, BB. *Blues on the Bayou*, CD. MCA Records, 1998.